GLACIER NATIONAL PARK
AFTER DARK

SUNSET TO SUNRISE IN A BELOVED MONTANA WILDERNESS

PHOTOGRAPHS & ESSAYS BY JOHN ASHLEY

THE FINE PRINT

Hard cover ISBN: 978-1-59152-178-5
Soft cover ISBN: 978-1-59152-160-0

Published by John Ashley Fine Art Photography
Layout and design by John Ashley
All images and text © 2015 John Ashley

Cover photo: "Silent Night." The winter Milky Way (left) and bright star Vega (center) shine through the fog over Lake McDonald, balancing Comet Lovejoy (right) as it rises above Mount Brown, in Glacier National Park.

"The Play" lyrics © Peter Mayer (http://www.petermayer.net/). Used with permission.

John Ashley Fine Art Photography
PO Box 855
Kila, MT 59920

Additional copies of this book, as well as fine art prints and Glacier National Park After Dark calendars, are available at: www.JohnAshleyFineArt.com.
For wholesale orders of John Ashley's books and calendars, please call Farcountry Press toll free at (800) 821-3874.

Produced by Sweetgrass Books.
PO Box 5630, Helena, MT 59604; (800) 821-3874; www.sweetgrassbooks.com.

The views expressed by the author/publisher in this book do not necessarily represent the views of, nor should be attributed to, Sweetgrass Books. Sweetgrass Books is not responsible for the content of the author/publisher's work.

Printed in China.

20   19   18   17   16   2   3   4   5   6

ACKNOWLEDGMENTS

I started this marathon alone and in the dark. But after years of working by myself, I needed a team to bring this long-term project into the light of day. Many over-educated friends and talented associates provided the encouragement, advice and proofreading skills needed to drag me across the finish line. Now some of these so-called friends are discussing ideas for a volume two even as I lie exhausted in the grass.

As a former coordinator of Montana's Indian Education For All program in Columbia Falls, Wendy Warren offered sage critique, like when I should ask for more advice. Editing insight and assistance were provided by long-time friend Amy Vanderbilt, the National Park Service's long-time Public Affairs Specialist at Glacier National Park. Fortunately, she underestimated the task when offering her proofreading services. My scientific verification team included the omniscient Jim Rogers, who teaches astronomy, physics and earth science for Salish Kootenai College. Retired University of Montana biology professor, Fred Allendorf, gently pointed out inconsistencies and mistakes in my early drafts without ever mentioning that he knows so much more than I do about pretty much everything. His enthusiasm for this project was infectious. I owe a huge debt of gratitude to Jack Gladstone, Montana's Blackfeet Troubadour and cultural bridge builder. Jack spent a good deal of time tracking down sources and explaining intricacies that cannot be divined through reading. His compassion for all cultures is an inspiration.

The kind ladies at Sweetgrass Books also provided invaluable assistance in getting these digital words and images onto paper. Kathy Springmeyer gently redirected my aim each time I painted outside the guidelines set by the publishing establishment. And Shirley Machonis was ever kind and passed no judgment while guiding a PC guy through the foreign MacIntosh world where book publishers work. Grammar was only a small part of my biology degree, so I'm immensely grateful to Caitlin Carroll for her artful editing.

All of these good people helped out in the production of this book. Any mistakes that slip into print remain the responsibility of the author.

I'd also like to make a point of thanking two total strangers, Mark Wagner and Ray Stinson. These two men are most responsible for getting the Dark Skies education program up and running in Glacier National Park, starting in 2009. National parks are perpetually underfunded and understaffed, especially on the ground, and I'm not sure that Glacier's Dark Skies program would have taken off without the efforts and passion of these men. Stinson and other astronomers set up telescopes hundreds of times to introduce more than 20,000 park visitors to the beauty overhead each summer, through viewing programs in Saint Mary and Apgar five nights a week, and daytime solar viewing opportunities in Apgar. In spite of pending budget cuts to this incredibly popular program, I hope the park finds the means to renew its support for many years to come.

Of course, I am indebted to my wife and business partner, Tracy, for her patience and encouragement over 20 years of my nighttime photography addiction. I suspect that my idiosyncrocies are easier to live with when I'm away on a fairly regular basis. Tracy runs our photography business and our energetic dogs while I'm out all night, and while I'm recovering over the next few days. She gently reminds me that it's not normal to drive 500 miles for a potential sky photograph just because it's cloudy here in the mountains. And yet, she is forever encouraging me to head out alone at night into prime grizzly bear habitat. Hmmm.

Finally, I thank you, dear reader. You picked this book up, and that's the first step to discovering a world at night that most of us have forgotten or maybe never even knew. If curiosity tugs at you as it does me, then subtle mysteries await you. All you need are a few keys to unlock the secrets of your own night vision. I hope you find them within these pages.

TABLE OF CONTENTS

Prologue 1

Sky Stories 2

Going-to-the-Sun ~
Staying for the Stars 5

Sunset, Alpenglow, Twilight
& the Golden Hour 6

The Belt of Venus 8

Moonrise in the Mountains 10

Old Chief ~ Governor of
the Mountains 13

Lunar Attraction 16

Chasing the Moon 18

One Summer Night 19

Night Visions 21

Aurora Borealis ~ Light of
the Northern Dancers 22

Air Glow Aurora 27

Milky Way Galaxy ~
The Wolf's Trail 28

Trails Across the Sky 32

Polaris ~ The Star
That Stands Still 35

Big Dipper ~ Seven Brothers
in the Great Bear 36

Orion in the Sky 39

Pleiades ~ The Lost Boys 40

A Star-Feeding 42

When Stars Fall 47

Dusty Stars & Snowballs 48

Near-Earth Asteroids 51

Wandering Planets, &
Son of Morning Star 52

Eclipsed Realities 54

Ursa Major Nocturne 57

Creatures of the Night 58

Mountain Moonsets 60

Solar Rays &
Moon Beams 66

Painting on Clouds 67

Returning to the Sun 68

Caution Lights & Progress 72

Bortle Scale Illustrations 74

Basics of Dark-Sky-
Friendly Lighting 78

Resources 79

Glacier National Park
Sky Events 2015–2024 80

A Shot in the Dark 82

Source Notes 84

Epilogue 90

"Watchtower." *The last rays of sunlight settle across the northwestern face of Chief Mountain, which is known to the Blackfeet as "Ninaistako" and to the Salish as "Silmtxʷcut." As the Sun reaches for the western horizon, night is getting ready to return to Glacier National Park.*

"Sunset at Last." *The last sunset of 2014 silhouettes the Huckleberry Mountain fire lookout and backlights a ridgeline of frost-covered trees. Visible on the sun's face are sunspots 2253 (left) and 2246 (right). (This image was made using an orange solar filter. <u>Never</u> point a telephoto lens at the sun unless the lens is properly filtered and you know what you are doing!)*

PROLOGUE

When I was an erratic young man, I met an elegant young woman in Glacier National Park where we both worked. On our first date we watched an odd parade walk up a gravel road, turn around, then walk back again to a rustic log cabin with its sagging front porch and creaking screen door. We melted into the glow of colorful locals inside the *Northern Lights Saloon*.

It was a good omen, and before long I was promising this woman the moon and stars. Eventually — and without pressing me for details — she accepted. This summer we're celebrating our 20th anniversary, and I'm finally making good on my promise.

Glacier National Park After Dark delivers the moon and stars — and the real-deal northern lights, comets and meteors, traditional native stories and more. It's a real life romance that takes place in Montana's most beloved wilderness, featuring heavenly bodies draped languidly across Glacier National Park's luscious landscapes. Like any graceful romance, most of the action takes place in the modesty of darkness.

The photographs in this book were born from more than 100 excursions into Glacier's darkness spanning almost 30 years. Nights spent in a wilderness are never boring. Unpredictable weather and untamed animals have a way of waking your dulled and domesticated senses. Localized, mountain-induced clouds are a common, radar-evading nemesis to night photography. Other challenges included -21F/-29C (battery-killing) temps during a comet, 40mph/64kph (tripod-shaking) wind during a winter eclipse, nosy (tripod-bumping) bighorn rams in moonlight, and an occasional grizzly bear passing in the night, to name a few from the following pages.

My own night photography in Glacier began one chilly morning in September 1987. That was the first time I talked a park ranger out of citing me for what looked to him like illegal camping. Parked along Lake McDonald, I was warming up in an idling car after spending six hours shivering next to a tripod to create my first photograph of stars blanketing the park's mountains. This scene turned into a re-run that played out again and again. I've met many curious park rangers and quizzical border patrol agents after midnight.

Back in 2001, some of the satellites that left thin white lines across my photographs also created the first atlas to measure our growing levels of artificial light.[1] Those maps from more than a decade ago, and a 2006 update, showed that 99% of continental U.S. residents already lived under artificial lights at night. In 2008, for the first time ever, more than half the world's population lived in cities.[2]

In the U.S., no untainted skies remain east of the Mississippi, and all but the brightest stars are lost to most Americans. Two-thirds of our grandparents can no longer see the Milky Way of their youth, and two-thirds of our children have never seen the Milky Way from their own backyards.[3] Without realizing it, we have slowly pulled modern curtains across our most ancient view. We traded a palette of Van Gough's stars for a nearly-barren night sky.

Glacier's Canadian sister, Waterton Lakes National Park, addressed the issue of light pollution in its 2008 release, *Guidelines and Specifications for Outdoor Lighting at Parks Canada*.[4] And just a few years ago, Glacier introduced an evening interpretive program in Saint Mary that is run by volunteer astronomers. In 2012, this "Dark Skies" program expanded to Apgar, and in 2014 more than 30,000 summer visitors bundled up to stand outside in dark parking lots and rediscover the nights' delights.[5]

Encouraged by the non-profit International Dark Sky Association, Waterton Lakes and Glacier are now working towards earning an International Dark Sky designation. We're starting to realize what's been lost elsewhere and learning to appreciate the dark night skies that we still have over most of Montana. We're gaining ground — or is it sky?

Glacier's visitation and appreciation grows each year. Out among the park's jagged mountains and forested valleys, taking good pictures in daylight is sort of like throwing rocks at the nearest planet — it's rather hard to miss no matter where you aim. Photography at night, however, is a different affair altogether. Chasing our dreams can run us ragged during the day. Night is where we lie still, turn introspective and wait to receive our personal visions. This difference, I think, is reflected in these photographs that were quietly crafted in the dark.

There are lots of good and genial trail guides living in the greater Glacier/Waterton area. But even by Montana standards they are all nominally-normal people who mostly snore at night. While they sleep it off, I've booked you on a nocturnal tour with a curious and cantankerous storyteller.

I'm Scots-Irish, not Blackfeet. I've only lived in these mountains for 30 years now. But in these pages I try to give voices to the people who have lived here for generations. The Blackfeet maintain more trails into their history than any others, so that is reflected here. My awe of Chief Mountain also shows up on many, many pages.

This way, please.

"Evening Reflections." *As the sunset slips down off the shoulders of Sinopah Mountain, a beaver emerges in Two Medicine Lake to begin his nocturnal work.*

Sky Stories

Glacier National Park straddles the Lewis and Livingston mountain ranges in northwestern Montana. But these are just modern names. The Blackfeet have a much older and more descriptive name for this region; *Miistakis*, the "Backbone-of-the-World." Native Americans have lived here along both sides of the Continental Divide for countless generations. They include three Blackfoot tribes along the eastern slopes (the *Pikuni* or Blackfeet, the *Kainai* or Blood, and the *Siksikau* or Blackfoot), and also the Kalispel (Flathead), Salish and Kootenai to the west.

All *Niitsitapi* or First Nations people[1] share their lives through storytelling and picture-writing.[2] These traditions form the breath and brush strokes of this book.

Modern tribes are working hard to maintain their oral traditions and revive their languages. They are once again teaching tribal histories and culture to children in their native tongue.[3] People living in the old buffalo (bison) country also told stories though picture-writing by painting glyph designs on the tanned black horn hides. Buffalo "story robe" paintings were personal records that documented important events.[4] "Winter count" paintings were tribal records that maintained group histories over many generations on a single buffalo hide.[5]

Winter counts were a memory calendar. Once each winter, a hieroglyph was added to the historical record. A council of men selected the event, and a respected historian, or *Ai Sinakinax*, drew the new glyph and memorized the new stories that, together, described that year.[6] These glyphs were often drawn in a chronological circle, and each drawing represented the year's most significant event. The longest surviving winter count, documenting 1764 through 1924, was maintained by four generations of Blackfeet men and one white missionary.[7] Currently, various records of 71 winter counts from Plains Indian tribes are known to still exist, including seven created by Blackfeet.[8] Many of these winter counts documented astronomical, night sky events.

Just like Europeans, the First Nations looked to the heavens to help them understand the world. "Sky People" (*spomi-tapi-ksi*) are an integral part of Blackfoot culture.[9] They are helpers who bridge the distance between the people and the "Source of Life," (*iihtsipaitapiiyo'pa*). Long ago the husband and wife team of Sun and Moon (*natosi* and *kokomi-kisomm*) provided the Blackfoot ancestors with teaching stories and sacred ceremonies to guide their generations.[10] Adults and children alike revel in these sky stories that the elders share only after dark.[11] The stories shared here are but one of many interpretations.[12]

We are a little less nomadic now, but you and I are still hunters and gatherers. We hunt for little nuggets of meaning, like the colorful pebbles

that we gather from the countless stones on Lake McDonald's shore. Humans have always been this way, but each one of us defines our own personal meaning in slightly different ways. We spend life filling our pocket with those nuggets that our spirit finds most attractive and comforting — our own prized collection of knowledge and faith. No two people or cultures carry the same pebbles.

There are more stars in the universe than pebbles on any beach, and sparkling night skies have also provided meaning and comfort. Night gives us the knowledge that every atom in our body was born in a star's heart, and our every cell is nursed by the sun through the plants and animals of this little planet. Night also provides the foundations for all of our comforting faiths and religions, supporting the narratives that help us navigate an honorable life of spiritual wonder. Reclaiming the night sky would reconnect us to our ancestors, nurture our health, and remind us of our humble position within the cosmos.

As we travel through the night from sunset to sunrise, I'll share stories on various subjects as we encounter them in the dark. At the end of each chapter I'll also offer a short suggestion about the topic at hand, starting with Sky Stories.

Write Your Own Sky Stories

The single most important action that you can take is this: *explore the darkest skies that are still available to you.* Maybe this means a camping trip to Glacier National Park. Maybe it's an occasional evening spent sky-watching in your own backyard with your children.

There are two sections in the back of this book, *Basics* and *Resources*, where I offer lighting tips and list some of the books and websites where you'll find specific information on lights, light shielding, and dark sky ordinances. This book shows you the beach, and groups like the International Dark Sky Association offer you the specific pebbles. Once you discover the night sky that belonged to your grandparents, you'll want to pass it on to your grandchildren. I'm sure of this.

"Blackfeet Warriors" (above). Moonlight sparkles in the eyes of a mounted warrior, poised to meet travelers at the northern border of the Blackfeet Reservation, on Glacier's east side. The steel sculptures were created by Blackfeet artist Jay Polite Laber using materials reclaimed from the 1965 flood.

"Spirit Above, Spirit Within" (facing page). The stars circle Polaris as Earth turns between dusk and dawn at a tepee sculpture overlooking the Saint Mary Valley.

"Kiss the Sun" (above). The sun kisses Chief Mountain while settling its way through thick clouds and behind the western horizon. Sunspot AR12192 is visible in several of the upper suns of this interval photograph, made using a solar filter. (Do not point a camera at the sun without the proper solar filter.)

"Sunspot AR12192" (facing page). Massive sunspot AR12192 made two laps around the sun in October and November of 2014 before fading back into the fire. It grew to about the same size as Jupiter, much wider than the Earth, and it was the largest sunspot since November 1990.[1]

Just like in your neighborhood, the sun dominates everything in Glacier National Park. Sunshine in the form of spring lupine leaves is recycled into muscular bighorn sheep living on Altyn Peak, in easy binocular range of the Many Glacier Campground.

Daylight also teases springtime glacier lilies, pulling them up through lingering July snowfields in the meadows around Logan Pass. Photosynthesis converts sunlight into energy (as carbohydrates), which is stored in the lilies' roots. Some of this solar energy will be dug up and eaten by what you might rightfully think of as solar-powered grizzly bears. And sun-feasting forbs, like clover, fattened up the Columbian ground squirrel that snatched jangled car keys away from surprised tourists who were trying to get a funny picture on the lawn at Apgar Village.[2]

It's a good idea to study the big map for a minute and get our bearings before sunset. The sun lies at the center of our neighborhood, providing us with a pretty good reason to call this place a solar system. Our home solar system contains eight planets — sorry, Pluto — plus several dwarf planets, dozens of planetary moons, one billion comets, and countless asteroids. The smaller stuff is rocky, icy debris left behind after the main construction phase. (We'll get to that stuff later on.) All of this is held together by gravity from the sun, which accounts for 99.86% of our solar system's mass.[3] But our sun is just one of the countless stars in space.

On a clear and moonless summer night at Cut Bank Creek (free of artificial, electric lights), you might count out 4,000 stars visible to your naked eyes, if you don't lose your place.[4] With very few exceptions, like the neighboring Andromeda galaxy, every single star that's visible to your unaided eye belongs to the luxurious Milky Way galaxy — our home sweet home.

Just like the Earth and sun, the Milky Way also spins. Flying through space at 490,000 miles per hour (220 km/sec), it takes our solar system 225 million years to complete one lap around the Milky Way.[5] But none of us will ever have to face turning 50 in cosmic years. The Earth itself has completed only 20 laps.

These days, Montana's "Big Sky" hangs *just so* between the Milky Way and Glacier National Park. This big, dark, night sky is our only window where we see and sense our place in the universe. It's a gentle reminder that we belong to the cosmos, not the other way around. Exploring the night sky in a Montana wilderness is not a loss of eyesight, but more like a re-awakening of insight. Our trip into real darkness isn't a journey of fear or dread, but rather an overdue homecoming, back to our original source of awe and wonder — the star-filled sky. You can spot bears in Many Glacier on any summer day. But night is the only time when you can watch the Great Bear (Ursa Major), shooting stars, the glowing Milky Way arching from east to west, or northern lights waving from the horizon. It's all still up there, but there are few places where we can still see it all.

Stars are round and smooth, but we always draw them with points. There are several

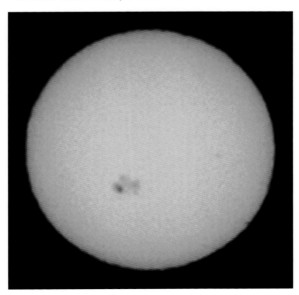

explanations for this visual contradiction. Stars look like they're twinkling because we're looking at them through an ocean of air that's in constant motion.[6] Different air densities flowing between your eyes and the stars is like changing eye-glasses, making the point of light dance around and bend into slightly different colors. Camera lenses and telescopes also bend light waves into diffraction spikes, which turn up in night time photographs. The iris inside a camera lens is the light-bending culprit, especially at smaller openings. Most telescopes have a second lens that's held in place by thin metal strips, and the incoming light bends around these strips to form spikes.[7] But even without cameras and telescopes, stars really do *appear* spiked to us because of imperfections in our eyes.

The lens inside each eyeball has tiny wrinkles that slightly bend round dots of light into pointed spikes before the light reaches our retina. The spike pattern differs between your two eyes, and your spike patterns are different from anyone else's.[8]

Sun Spotting in Glacier

If you have difficulty locating the sun in Glacier, don't worry. That just means it's winter. Or perhaps June, our rainiest month. On those glorious days when the clouds part and our resident star makes an appearance, you must remember to be polite and <u>never</u> stare. The lens in your eye would focus that energy and fry your retina like a magnifying glass over an ant. That goes double when using a camera, triple with a telephoto lens (unless using a solar filter).

When you reach your hand to the sky and trace the sun's path from east to west, you're drawing the ecliptic, the curved path that the sun follows across Glacier's sky. On June's summer solstice our sun rises at 40 degrees northeast and sets at 294 degrees northwest, an ecliptic that's 254 degrees wide. On December's winter solstice, the sun appears at 111 degrees southeast and departs at 221 degrees southwest, an arced path of just 110 degrees — less than one-half of the summer ecliptic!

SUNSET, ALPENGLOW, TWILIGHT & THE GOLDEN HOUR

I felt sufficiently handsome and immortal at 18. Subsequent years have proved me wrong on both accounts, and nowadays I'm gray-bearded and much more introspective. Like my own mortality, the transition between day and night is tenuous. This brief but handsome transition includes sunset, alpenglow, twilight and the so-called "golden hour."

Sunset aficionados might divide their favorite time of day into three parts — any excuse to linger. The first part is sunset proper. The sun is visible but touching the horizon, and sunlight still reaches most things above the horizon. Most of the sky is still blue.

The second part of sunset begins when the sun drops below the horizon. Sunlight passing through lots of atmosphere loses most of its blue wavelengths, leaving red light. This colors the clouds and the countless tiny, invisible particles floating in the air. The clouds and atmosphere reflect a reddish-orange color upon the mountains. Technically speaking, it is this indirect, reflected light painting the mountains and sky that is the true alpenglow.

Finally, the third part of sunset is the last bit of warm color before the cool-blue night. By now, only the clouds are colored by reflected light, and all of Glacier's mountains are in blue shadow.

That's just one of many descriptions for sunset. The Earth still spins regardless of your chosen terminology, and most of us use "alpenglow" to describe any colorful light in the mountains or sky that you see around sunset (and sunrise).

Twilight, on the other hand, is the technical term for sunset. It's still just the transition between day and night, when your location is lit by sunlight reflected down from the upper atmosphere. But twilight has three precisely defined periods.[1]

Civil twilight is the period when the sun's center is between 0 and 6 degrees below the level horizon. Most planets and the brightest stars begin showing up during civil twilight, and there's still enough light to clearly see the horizon.

Nautical twilight is the period when the sun's center is between 6 and 12 degrees below the horizon. You can still see general outlines but some objects might be hard to distinguish. On moonless nights, this was the last chance for old-time mariners to see the horizon well enough to use a sextant for measuring angles to the stars above (the origin of its name).

Finally, astronomical twilight is the period when the sun's center is between 12 and 18 degrees below the horizon. During this time, scattered sunlight in the atmosphere is barely brighter than the faintest stars. In other words, the dimmest stars only become visible after evening's astronomical twilight passes into night. And speaking of dim...

The "golden hour" is a yellow sticky note that photographers slap against their foreheads. It's just a mental reminder that the best light for landscape photography usually lasts for less than one hour, centered around sunset (and sunrise).

That's when the light around us is reddish-orange, with softer shadows and less contrast, and looks generally pleasing. Under identical cloud conditions, the golden hour lasts longer in winter than in summer. That's because the winter sun breaks the horizon at a more oblique angle, and the summer sun arrives and departs at a steeper angle. Yes, there's an app for that.[2]

Get Ready for Alpenglow

When in Rome, watch Romans. When you're in Montana, you'll want to watch the mountains. Alpenglow appears most often on clear and cloudless evenings (mornings, too). If the sky looks promising, watch the highest mountaintops on the horizon opposite from the sunset. Lower mountains are often shaded by taller peaks when alpenglow appears. Be patient and be ready. Alpenglow might only last a few moments.

"North Fork Alpenglow." *The sun's last direct rays color the cliffs on Vulture Peak in the North Fork Valley. The Kootenai called this mountain* Nahsukin, *but mapmakers moved this original name to the next peak eastward. No origin is known for the current name of Vulture Peak.*[3]

"Mount Reynolds" (top). Evening's last direct sunbeams spotlight Mount Reynolds, which was named by G.B. Grinnell for another editor of Field & Stream magazine.[4]

"Blackfeet Alpenglow" (above). Color in the clouds and sky reflect nicely on Mount Jackson, as viewed from the North Fork. G.B. Grinnell gave the mountain its current name, but William McClintock knew it as Blackfeet Mountain.[5]

"Fire on the Water" (right). After sunset, backscattered sunlight paints the clouds orange above Stanton Mountain and Mount Vaught, and reflects in Lake McDonald. The Kootenai name for Mount Vaught is "Big Old Man."[6]

THE BELT OF VENUS

There isn't much shade in space, mostly just the cone-shaped shadows hiding behind planets. Day and night lose their earthly meanings when viewed from out there. Space is black and sunlight is white. So then why does Glacier's "Big Sky" look blue, yellow, orange or pink?

Our midday sky looks blue because of the way our atmosphere interacts with sunlight. What we call "sky" is mostly a thin ocean of invisible atoms, gas molecules and dust. When white light strikes a large molecule, all of its component colors react the same way, and it remains white (Mie scattering). But when white light strikes tiny particles, the component colors react differently (Rayleigh scattering).[1]

Think of a rainbow, which is white light separated into the six colors (wavelengths) that our eyes can detect. You have longer wavelengths at one end (red, orange, yellow) and shorter wavelengths at the other end (green, blue, violet). The red end of this spectrum has wavelengths that are longer than most air molecules, so reds pass through unaffected. The blue end has shorter wavelengths, and these "bounce" or scatter off air particles about 9.4 times more often.[2] So when it comes to sky colors, size matters.

When we look overhead, our eyes are catching the scattered blue wavelength. When we look towards the sun we see less of the scattered light, and the white sun now appears yellow. When the sun is near the horizon at sunset or sunrise, we are looking though so much atmosphere that blue, green and yellow waves are all scattered away, leaving only red and orange. Some summers we also see daytime red skies over Glacier National Park. During active fire seasons, particles of smoke also scatter the blues away, leaving us with "angry" red skies.

Okay, then why doesn't the daytime sky look violet instead of blue? Because the cone cells in our eyes work more efficiently with blue than with violet.[3] So which is reality, the blue that we see or the violet that's really there?

If you turn and face away from the sunset, you are standing at one rim of a party-hat-shaped shadow, the cone that we call night. When viewed from either rim (sunset or sunrise), Earth's dark blue shadow is called the "twilight wedge."[4] Just after you reach this point, if the clouds cooperate, there's an ephemeral sky beauty who might make a cameo appearance. When conditions are just right, a glowing arc of pinkish light forms between the twilight wedge and light blue sky. This narrow band of pinkish color is called the "Belt of Venus." The names comes from Greek mythology, not our sister planet.

Venus' belt might show up as a thin layer of brown or salmon or pink. This layer is always near the horizon that's opposite the sun; west in the morning, east in the evening. The belt forms and fades in 15 minutes or less, and it usually goes unnoticed because we're watching the sun instead. Earth doesn't stand still to admire this moment, and as you revolve you're looking through more and more wedge until you are deep inside the shadow. A better name for our human soap opera might be, "The Wedge of Night."

The Belt of Venus is at its best when the sky is clear of clouds, but the atmosphere is a little bit dusty or smoky. The belt's color comes to us as back-scattered sunlight. The sun is on the horizon about 100 miles east or west of your location, but it's still shining on the atmosphere 50–100 miles away from you in the opposite direction.[5] The longer, redder light that's left strikes the dusty bits and bounces back to your eyes.

Let's play "what if" with our blue "Big Sky." We're familiar with the emotional effects that different colors create in our brains. We paint our children's nurseries in soothing shades of "baby blues" and pinks, never red. But what if the physics of light were just a tad different and we evolved under a bright red sky? Would red be our comforting color? Would the appearance of a less-familiar blue color raise our heart rates? Would we see a soothing red sky and an angry blue sunset? It's something to mull over while waiting for Venus to find her belt.

Look for the Belt of Venus

You might catch a glimpse of Venus' wardrobe accessories whenever the skies are clear over Glacier for sunrise or sunset. Watch for her to appear in the west at dawn, in the east at dusk. If there are clouds lurking about, then she'll probably remain demurely hidden from view.

| Twilight | +5 minutes | +10 minutes | +15 minutes | +20 minutes | +25 minutes | +30 minutes |

"Belt of Venus Illustration." In this example photographed at dawn, the Belt of Venus colors appear at +10 minutes and are just about gone at +25 minutes, a total of 15 minutes. The Belt's height and color varies. Scattered blue skylight begins filling the sky, and scattered yellow light is visible on the horizon.

"Belted Sky" (left). A faint Belt of Venus forms over the Livingston Range on Glacier's west side. The Earth's twilight wedge is visible below the back-scattered, pink light.

"Divide Moonrise" (below). The full moon climbs up Divide Mountain's eastern flank, through Venus' belt above the Saint Mary Valley. Divide Mountain is held sacred by the Blackfoot, and their traditional name for it is "Mountain-from-which-the-Water-goes-to-the-Behind-Direction-and-to-the-South-Direction."[6]

MOONRISE IN THE MOUNTAINS

A traditional Blackfoot story tells of the long-ago time when Moon Woman rose up and left the Earth.[1] She bore a mysterious black birthmark on one calf that almost led to her undoing.

She had lived here before, married a Blackfoot man and bore him two sons. But she fell in love with a handsome Star that she met while collecting firewood. The woman eventually left her Earthly family to climb into the sky as the Moon so she could marry this Star. After some time she began missing her two sons, and she asked her husband if she could return to visit them. The Moon and Star disguised themselves as men and climbed down to the father's lodge.

The father and two sons were suspicious but took the strangers in and treated them kindly. The smaller man seemed especially affectionate towards the boys, hugging and kissing them. The father kept these men up long into the night, telling them many stories so they would be very tired and sleep soundly. Late in the night he crept over and lifted the robe to reveal the stranger's leg. When he saw the black birthmark, he knew this stranger was his ex-wife in disguise.

The next morning the father sent his sons outside, but he blocked the doorway so the strangers could not leave. He lashed out at the woman for leaving her family, and he threatened them both with his flint knife. Just as he lunged, the Moon and Star flew up through the smoke flaps like crackling sparks from the campfire and escaped back into the sky. On nights when the sky is clear, you can still see a dark birthmark on the Moon.

Normally when the moon visits us during the day, we see only a sunlit crescent because the sky is too bright and outshines the moon's unlit portion. But when the timing and conditions are just right at sunset and sunrise, we can see the rest of the moon glowing in twice-reflected light. Earthshine is sunlight that reflects off the Earth's sunny side onto the moon's dark face, and then reflects back to us. This glow is brightest when the moon is low on the horizon, and the sunlit part of Earth has lots of fresh snow or light clouds. The portion of sunlight that reflects off the Earth is known as its albedo. Snow and clouds are the most reflective (35–95%) while forests and oceans are least reflective (5–15%).

An Earthshine-lit crescent moon is sometimes called the old moon in the new moon's cradle. Reflect backwards when you see Earthshine. If you were looking back from the middle of the moon's visible disc, Earth would appear almost full with just a thin crescent of darkened shadow.

Earthshine in Glacier

Because Earthshine depends partly on weather conditions to our west, it's almost impossible to predict when we'll be able to see it from Glacier. Your best chance to see Earthshine is to make a habit of keeping your eye on the moon, especially when she's near the horizon. You just never know what she might do.

"Moonlit Rain" (above). A full moon rises through a twilight rain over the shoulders of Divide Mountain.
"Earthshine Moon" (top). Sunlight reflecting off Earth lights up the unlit portion of a crescent moon. This is sometimes called the old moon in the new moon's cradle.

"Mount Saint Nicholas Moonrise." *A March full moon glows through thin clouds while rising above the shoulders of Mount Saint Nicholas, along the park's southern edge. The Kootenai call this mountain* Kasinquwa, *or "Two Feathers." For this photograph I climbed a steep ridge on snowshoes to reach my calculated camera location, and about an hour later the moon rose right on target.*

"Chief Mountain Moonrise." *The full moon rises up and passes behind Chief Mountain. This in an interval photograph, and the moon images were taken two minutes apart. Combining the images in-camera shows us the path that the moon took across the sky.*

OLD CHIEF ~ GOVERNOR OF THE MOUNTAINS

Chief Mountain transcends our modern way of thinking about place and time. The mountain is a sacred area, the setting for the Blackfoot creation story and the home of Thunderbird. This monolithic mountain is revered by people of many cultures, myself included.

Old Chief, as it's known north of the border, is an upside-down mountain. The 600-million-year-old cap rocks rest upon layers of much younger rocks, one result of the Lewis Overthrust Belt. The highest rocks hold fossils from some of the oldest-known lifeforms on Earth.[1]

There are many traditional stories associated with Old Chief. My favorite comes from north of the border.[2] It's a story that you seldom hear, but I think of it every time I want to photograph the Old Chief but he is shrouded in clouds.

As the old story goes, a great chief owned a herd of magnificent white horses that roamed the mountain. Only his daughter knew the secret path to the top, and he always left her in charge of the horses whenever he was away hunting.

But she had spurned a young man who now wanted revenge, so he spied to learn her secret. While the chief was away, the young man led an enemy band up the mountain to steal the horses. When the daughter saw them approaching, she mounted her favorite snow-white horse. The enemy closed off her only escape route just as a snowstorm engulfed the mountain. She pushed her horse into a gallop and raced the entire herd into the storm. The enemy followed, and they all disappeared over the cliffs.

Whenever Blackfoot see snow swirling around Old Chief, they say, *"White horses rise swift and high."*

Between 1791 and 1822, a young British cartographer named Peter Fidler traveled more than 47,000 miles (75,640 km) by foot, horseback and canoe while mapping the northern Rocky Mountains.[3] During the winter of 1792, Fidler met a Pikuni Blackfeet named The Feathers. The two men did not speak a common language, but, using a charred stick on a buffalo hide, The Feathers helped Fidler by drawing out the northern Missouri River headwaters and drainages. Fidler sent his accumulated information back to his employer, the Hudson Bay Company, which forwarded the notes on to a London mapmaker, Aaron Arrowsmith. In 1795, Arrowsmith produced the first map to name the sacred mountain. Fidler called it "The King,"[4]

...called by these Indians Nin nase tok que or the King & by the Southern Indians the Governor of the Mountain, being the highest known place they know of...[5]

On June 5, 1805, another roving band spotted Chief Mountain from a campsite 100 miles to the east, near the Sweetgrass Hills. Their leader plotted it with the name "Tower Mountain."[6] On July 22, 1806, these same explorers camped again within sight of Chief Mountain. Their leader compared his view to the copy of Arrowsmith's incomplete map, with confounding additions made to it in 1802.[7] When he aimed his sextant at the north star, he realized that the headwaters did not go beyond 50 degrees north latitude, as hoped.[8] Discovering no easy route across the mountains, Meriwether Lewis turned his band back southward without ever entering the mountains that would later become Glacier National Park.

Respect For Your Elders

Many years ago a Blackfeet friend invited me to join him on his annual pilgrimage to the summit of Chief Mountain. This was a high honor, but I declined. How I would love to experience the mountain that I've admired from a distance for decades! But as I explained to him, "I'm a white guy. It's a sacred site. I don't *need* to go there."

There are times when we should curb our own desires to honor the beliefs and needs of other cultures. Sacred sites should not become tourist playgrounds, and no one's church should be desecrated by industry. Chief Mountain should always be treated as a sacred Blackfoot area.

"Old Chief's Family." Comet Lovejoy (C/2014 Q2) fades into the clouds in January 2015 above Chief Mountain (right), his wife Ninaki Mountain (center) and their small child, Papoose Mountain (left).

"Old Chief Milky Way." Chief Mountain watches the Milky Way as it moves past just after midnight. Pink color in the clouds is partly from a crescent moon just below the horizon and partly from outdoor security lights in Babb.

"Chief Mountain Moonset." *A full moon sets into the colorful Belt of Venus just before dawn behind Chief Mountain.*

LUNAR ATTRACTION

The moon is a little younger than Earth. But a hard life has left it wrinkled and dusty like a favorite crazy uncle.

Most of our moon was once a chunk of Earth. About 4.53 billion years ago, a proto-planet the size of Mars smacked into what was still a mostly molten Earth. Lighter mantle material from the Earth's surface splashed out into orbit around our young planet, while most of the Earth's heavier metals remained behind, sunk deep in its core. Most of this ejected material formed a ring around Earth (sort of like Saturn's rings) before the debris eventually collided and coalesced into *two* moons, one large and one small. Both moons settled into orbit around Earth.[1]

Can you contemplate the sight of two moons from Boulder Pass, Glacier's highest campsite? Then imagine watching this: gravity slowly dislodged the smaller moon from its comfortable orbit. It caught up and crumpled into its larger brother in a low-speed collision that left behind Everest-size mountains.[2]

Now we have one moon that's about 27% of Earth's diameter, with a cratered half that we see and a mountainous half that we don't see (the "dark" or far side). It has no global magnetic field, just patches of weakly-magnetized surface rocks.[3] It's mostly composed of lighter Earth crust and with only 1.2% of the Earth's mass, which helps to explain why it only has 17% as much gravity.[4]

Gravity is what holds a thin layer of atmosphere tight to Earth's surface. The moon's weak gravity can only hold onto a much thinner atmosphere. But meteorite impacts can create temporary lunar clouds of water vapor, and over the eons some of this vapor has re-condensed into surface ice, hidden away in deep, cold (-243F/-153C) and permanently-dark south pole craters.[5]

We think of tides as the moon's gravitational pull on oceans. But tides distort the entire shapes of large bodies near to each other. Tides also pull and distort solid rock, and this attraction go both ways between the Earth and the moon.

The moon's gravity lifts our flexible oceans about 3 feet (1 meter) twice a day in the open ocean. The sea floor and coastline shapes can magnify this tidal effect up to 59 feet (18 meters). The moon's tidal forces also lift the Earth's crust, and these solid rock "body tides" rise up about 7.8 inches (20 cm) twice a day. Your body, too, is taller when the moon is high overhead, by about 1/1,000th the diameter of a single atom.[7]

The Earth also causes body tides on the moon, lifting the moon's crust by 4 inches (10 cm).[8] By comparison, Jupiter's massive tidal force lifts the surface of its moon, Io, by *several hundred feet* during each moon rotation. This generates a tremendous amount of internal heat and keeps Io cooking as the most volcanically active body in our solar system.[9]

Friction caused by Earthly tidal distortions on the solid moon slowed the moon's spin until it matched its orbital period around us. The moon is now "tidally locked" to Earth. The moon rotates once on its axis every 23.7 days as it revolves once around the Earth during this period. That's why we always see the same moon face.[10]

The sun has 27 million times more mass than the moon but is 400 times further away, and its tidal effects on the Earth are only half as strong.[6] Mass and distance have a complicated, inverse cube relationship on gravity. The effects on Earth from any other planetary alignments are infinitesimal.

One Earth day was just 18.9 hours long 900 million years ago.[11] But the energy used for Earth's rotation is also getting used for body tide distortion, internal heat generation, and ocean tide friction. These forces are slowing down the Earth's rotation, which in turn pushes the moon into a higher and faster orbit. Over a 100-year span, our Earth days grow 0.0023 seconds longer. And each year the moon moves 1.5 inches (3.8 cm) further away.[12]

These combined effects over billions of years will add up to a much different lunar sight. Our moon will move about twice as far away (no more total

solar eclipses!). One Earth day and one lunar month will become synchronized at a length of 47 current Earth days, and the moon will appear fixed in place in our sky.[13] This is already the case for most of the moons orbiting our largest planets (Jupiter, Saturn, Uranus, Neptune), as George Darwin (son of Charles) first explained in 1879.[14]

Earth is the only local planet that clings to a single moon. Mars is close with two moons, and ancient moons apparently crashed into both Venus and Mercury, leaving them moonless. But under current definitions (which change) the other planets are buzzing with moons. Neptune has 14, and Uranus is next with 27. Saturn and Jupiter are credited with 62 and 67 moons, respectively.[15] Planetary gravity can also pull in comets and asteroids that become temporary moons. A 15-foot (5 meter) asteroid orbited Earth four times during 2006–2007 before getting tossed back out into space.[16]

Lunar Viewing

When Glacier National Park was dedicated in 1910, the moon was more than 13 feet (4 m) closer than it is today. It will never be closer, so now is a good time for you to view the moon from Glacier, and to visit that crazy old uncle.

"Mount Reynolds Moon" *(above). The full moon passes through the evening sky above Mount Reynolds. This in an interval photograph, and the moon images were recorded two minutes apart. I had to stand guard over my tripod during this image to keep a nosey bighorn ram away from the camera.*

"Cloudy Moon" *(facing page). We often see the full moons of summer in the northern Rockies. But the full moons during the rest of our year are often draped or completely hidden in clouds, which makes them that much more mysterious.*

CHASING THE MOON

The first time I lined the moon up behind something, anything, I used an old Montana road atlas, a pencil and a ruler. My methodology proved to be slightly more accurate than the next-best option I knew of at the time, throwing darts at the map. This was a long time ago, probably before you were born, back when the internet was new and the only data available were sun and moon charts from the U.S. Naval Observatory.

For this first alignment I measured the angles, distances and elevations, and settled on a point in an old clear cut on the Forest Service side of the North Fork Road. It was about a half-mile hike in from the Demers Ridge trailhead. I lugged 40 pounds of camera gear, lenses and tripod to a spot that I estimated to be the point I'd circled on my paper map. After setting up my biggest lens (back then, a 300mm with a 2x converter) I settled in and waited for the evening moon to rise behind the fire lookout on top of Huckleberry Mountain.

I'd figured out a secret, or at least something I hadn't realized before, and now I was putting it to a real-life test. If I stood next to the lookout and photographed the moon, the lookout would look big and the moon small. If I backed up some distance, they'd both look the same size. And if I backed up several miles, with the lookout still visible, then the moon would look huge. No matter where I go with one lens, the moon will be the same size in every photo. But I can grow the moon by shrinking the lookout. It wasn't some trick, it was real-life geometry. All I had to do was simply line things up.

Now here's the problem with mountains — they're crooked. I owned paper charts showing the moonrise azimuths, times, etc., but the azimuth (compass direction in degrees) assumes that you have a perfectly level horizon. If there's a mountain in the way, it shifts where the moon breaks the horizon because it rises and sets at an angle — that curved ecliptic.

On the first evening the moon broke the horizon just a couple of widths to the right, or west of the lookout. I recalculated and returned the next day. On my second attempt, the moon slowly climbed up the ridge towards the lookout, but missed by half a moon's width to the left. I had moved my camera location about 50 yards to the east, just a tad too far. Recalculating. On the third evening, I moved east just a skosh more. My heart rate rose with the moon, and I broke into a silent jig when it slipped behind the lookout — careful to step back from the tripod first. Yesssss!

The Moon Illusion

The moon illusion is the oldest visual trick of them all. Philosophers and scientists have thrown theories at it for 3,000 years but none have stuck.[1] Simply put, the moon (or sun or a constellation) looks larger and closer when near the horizon than when higher up in the sky. The average mis-estimate is 50-75% larger.[2] This illusion is strictly perceptual, our brain's own Gordian Knot of tangled interpretations. One version goes like this: we *perceive* the sky as closer than the horizon because a cloud looks much larger overhead than it does after it has moved to the horizon. When the moon is viewed together with landscape near the horizon, we *perceive* it to be further away, like the cloud. Because it is *perceived* as further away, the brain up-sizes the visual interpretation. And then we *perceive* the moon to be closer because it's up-sized. But cognitive psychologists tell us that perceptions can't cause perceptions, so we're back to where we started.[3] Stare into the next moonrise and maybe you'll be the one to untangle the long-running moon illusion.

"Huckleberry Moon." *A mid-summer full moon rises past the Huckleberry Mountain fire lookout. This image required three attempts to line the moon up with the fire lookout.*

ONE SUMMER NIGHT

One night many summers back, I found myself sitting beside my tripod on a gravelly lake-shore while my camera clicked off one image every 30 seconds, as programmed. A full moon slowly sank behind Apgar Village (page 60). With so much time to think, I was running out of ideas.

I stared out across a moonlit Lake McDonald, over to the Fish Creek Campground and picnic area. Hmmm. The gears started grinding as I tried to triangulate in my mind. If I was over *there*, and the moon's over *there*, and the wind dies down again, can I capture the whole arc from moonrise to moonset? I was back before sunset, measuring angles and setting up my tripod at the picnic area (page 83), when a couple of young campers walked down to skip stones on the lake.

"What are you taking pictures of?" they asked. My camera was sitting on a tripod at water's edge.

"Nothing yet," I answered. *"But at sunset the full moon will rise right over there,"* (pointing left across the lake to the Belton Hills), *"and eventually it'll set over here"* (pointing right towards the slopes of Apgar Mountain).

Momentary silence. *"You mean, you're going to stand out here all night?"* It was a fair question.

"Well, yeah," I answered. *"Almost. The moon sets around four. Then I'll go home."*

They didn't say another word. Instead, both of them backed slowly away from the crazy guy with a camera. I spent the next six hours walking in circles, scribbing notes, and hoping that the ranger on duty didn't show up in the middle of the night to blind me with his flashlight and shine it all over my camera set up.

"Lake McDonald Pearls." The full moon's path across the night sky above Lake McDonald is reflected on a rare, windless evening. The moon rises on the left at about 10 p.m. and sets on the right at 3:45 a.m., and the moon was photographed every five minutes. The images were then combined in-camera.

"Green and Blue." *On a moonless night over Saint Mary, 2014's Comet Lovejoy (C/2014 Q2) visits the blue nebula surrounding the Pleiades, the six Lost Boys of Blackfoot legends. Lovejoy's green coma is created by diatomic carbon fluorescing in ultraviolet light in the near-vacuum of space.*

NIGHT VISIONS

We like to call Montana the "Big Sky" state, but this nickname must be rooted on the eastern plains where they have 180-degree views. Here in western Montana, we're surrounded by mountains like cedar saplings in an old-growth forest.

Mountains raise our horizons up above eye level, narrow the visible "Big Sky" by 10–20 degrees and lift our gaze skyward. No, the awe-inspiring peaks of Glacier National Park are more like the "Last Best Place" (another Montana nickname) that forms a rustic picture frame around the night sky.

We don't just see photographs of stars and comets, we *feel* them. They rouse your synapses like memories of your first campfire that you sort-of remember, vaguely but fondly. Why do night images affect us this way? It's something in our genes. Or more precisely, something in our eyes.

You might remember learning about rods and cones in school. They're two types of light-sensitive cells in your eyes. But what your teachers probably didn't tell you is that, in the shade of night, your eyes lie. Rods and cones evolved through activity in daylight, when we're most active. At night, our eyes slack off and tell us to move along, there's nothing to see "out there."

Rod cells are sensitive to dim light levels ("scotopic" vision), but they don't see color. On the other hand, cone cells see colors but they only work in bright light ("photopic" vision). When it comes to seeing in the dark, this combination is like putting eye-poking Curly and Moe in charge of safety. Between the two numbskulls, a brilliant sky filled with colorful stars looks like a dark ceiling with a handful of dim specks. To see in the dark, you need to take control of your inner stooge.

Step outside at night in Whitefish (a small town near Glacier), and you'll be lucky to count a dozen stars overhead. Stand around in the shadows for 20 minutes and — if a curious cop doesn't show up first — a couple dozen stars will eventually appear. Glance at your bright cell phone before looking up again, and suddenly you're back to less than a dozen stars. The same thing happens when you drive into Glacier at night with your headlights on, which I strongly recommend. Wait for 20 minutes in Glacier's darkness, and you'll discover at least 3,000 glimmering stars waiting.

This is our ancient night vision — a forgotten skill. Rods and cones use chemicals to convert photons into electrical messages that the brain can understand. But bright light uses up these chemicals faster than our cones can replenish them. We need 20–60 minutes of darkness to refuel our eyes for night viewing. Astronomers and the odd photographer wear red headlamps, not white, because red light doesn't deplete these eye chemicals or dim our night vision. Red headlamps also have the added feature of making techno-geeks look really, really cool.

We know lots of cool things about rods and cones. But like Larry, the serious stooge, we know a lot less about our third eye.

In addition to rods and cones, we have a third type of light-sensitive cell in our eyes, in our retinas, called retinal ganglion cells (RGC).[1] These microscopic cells have a huge effect when humans and light meet. RGCs regulate the production of melatonin by sending signals to our pineal gland, perched near the middle of our brains like some mysterious portal between two lumpy hemispheres. Our pineal gland, skin and eyes are the only organs that are light sensitive.

Named for its pinecone shape, the brain's pineal gland is so dedicated to light that it was once considered to be a third eye. The gland has just one function. When RGCs in our eyes detect darkness, the pineal gland secretes melatonin. That's it. Melatonin is a hormone with three rather important functions. It controls our circadian body functions, regulates our reproductive hormones, and keeps cancer cells from growing. When it's dark, we produce melatonin. When it's light, not so much.[2]

Over millions of years, our bodies evolved to be alert during one bright day shift that's followed by one drowsy, dark night shift. Electric lighting broke this natural cycle and chained us to a new, artificial economy, with 24 hours of man-made "daylight" and little or no old-fashioned darkness left over. Even faint artificial light at night is detected by our third eye, which suppresses melatonin production and messes with our brains.[3] How scrambled are we? Sleep disorders, headaches, fatigue, obesity, anxiety, and several kinds of cancers (including breast and colon cancers) are just some of the health problems now tied to artificial light at night.[4,5,6]

Like incandescent light bulbs, we first thought that the light-emitting diode (LED) revolution was a godsend. It was, in the sense of energy conservation. But LEDs attract nearly 50% more insects,[7] and most LEDs produce the very wavelength that's most disruptive to melatonin production (blue light between 430 and 510nm). Now engineers are working to develop LEDs with less blue and more red wavelengths that will be less damaging to human health.[8,9]

The mysterious pineal gland has been described as a "blind spot in Western rationality." It's suspected — but not yet proven — to contribute to the wild visual effects that we experience during dreams, religious visions, and other altered states.[10] I wouldn't be surprised, considering my own lunar madness. My wife thinks that I reside in an altered state. I simply know it as "Montana."

Rediscover Your Visions

More than 40% of the U.S. population now lives where real darkness no longer exists. Artificial light levels exceed the glow of a full moon, and in these conditions human eyes never switch to scotopic, or night vision. But scotopic vision is required to see the Milky Way, most northern light displays, and many comets. The only path to night vision requires finding old-fashioned darkness and avoiding white light for 20–60 minutes. Averted vision also works well. The less-sensitive cone cells are most dense near the center of your retina. To see faint objects, use more of your light-sensitive rod cells by looking 10–15 degrees off-center, toward your nose.

AURORA BOREALIS ~ LIGHT OF THE NORTHERN DANCERS

Pierre Gassendi might just be the most influential French priest and philosopher that you've never heard of. Twenty-eight years younger than Galileo, Gassendi was an early promoter of empiricism. He argued that knowledge required sensory-based evidence, not untestable and unprovable beliefs. His arguments ran counter to the ancient Greeks and church dictates of his time. But Gassendi's work lent credence to scholars like Nicolaus Copernicus, who booted Earth (and thus man) from the center of the universe.[1]

In 1621, Gassendi was also the man who attached the Greek names of Aurora and Borealis to the northern lights. Aurora was the Roman goddess of dawn and Boreas the god of the north wind. The ancient Chinese and Greeks had older names for northern lights, but it's *aurora borealis* that sticks with us today. And these days it's Gassendi's empirical version of science that guides our management of park service lands.

Along Glacier National Park's eastern side, the traditional Blackfeet call this glow *Apatohsitapi aipitskiaiw*,[2] or "Light of the Northern Dancers." It's taken as a sign that a violent wind will soon arrive.[3] You're well-versed in the ways of the wind if you've spent any time on Glacier's east side. (I once asked a woman if the wind always blows hard in Babb. Not always, she said, but if it stops everyone falls over.)

Northern lights form a continuous oval around Earth's poles. Sometimes they roll south and become visible in Montana. Most of the auroras we see here begin with a case of solar indigestion. The sun blows a constant breeze of solar wind in all directions. Earth's magnetic field reaches out into space and acts like a windbreak that redirects these charged electrons around our planet. In the process, this magnetic field gets compressed on Earth's sunlit side and elongated on the downwind or night side, like a wiggling tadpole facing the sun.

Every few days the sun's roiling surface cuts loose with an enormous cosmic belch, blowing a stream of plasma and ions into space at 900,000 mph (400 km/sec). When this plasma bubble is pointed in the right direction, it will collide with Earth's magnetosphere 2–3 days later. Electrons then follow these far-reaching magnetic waves down into our atmosphere. Solar electrons strike atmospheric gases, and these "excited" atoms burn off the extra energy as visible light and return to their previous electrical and invisible states. The color produced depends on the kind of atom that is struck.

Our most common green aurora occurs when the fast-moving electrons run into oxygen atoms 60–100 miles (95–160 km) high. A pink or crimson lower edge means that electrons are striking nitrogen molecules at around 60 miles (95 km) altitude. More rarely, red is produced by oxygen atoms at upper altitudes of 185–250 miles (300–400 km). Blue and purple northern lights can also shine from hydrogen and helium atoms, respectively, but these colors are hard for our eyes to detect.[4]

Because the aurora borealis is tied to magnetic fields, it's mostly a polar phenomenon. Montana's a little more than halfway from the equator to the north pole, and we see the dancing lights about half as often as people living in the Canadian provinces to our north. High-latitude locations don't turn completely dark in mid-summer, but their winter nights are extra long. That's why northern lights are sometimes mistakenly thought of as winter events. Auroras aren't, they just show up better when the dance floor lights are dimmed.

People watched auroras long before recorded history (except for a handful of cultures that feared them and hid). But it wasn't until the late 1950s that scientists coordinated their efforts to understand the lights better. More than 100 all-sky cameras were set up in different locations to study the same aurora at the same time. Analysis of these data illuminated two new concepts, the auroral oval and the auroral sub-storm.[5]

Many people had noticed that auroras tend to appear first along the northern horizon, pulsing southward and then fading back north again as the night progressed. It often began as a diffuse arc, growing active around midnight, then fading before dawn. The cameras revealed that the aurora seen in various locations was really one huge and continuous oval.[6]

When the diffuse aurora becomes active around midnight, localized patches break into curtains that expand north and south. These pulsating waves are the auroral sub-storms, the music that makes the colorful sheets and rays want to get up and dance. The dancing usually dissipates before dawn.

Space scientists recently discovered that some auroras have a different cause — wrinkles in the Earth's magnetic field. Occasionally, a gravitational bow wave snaps, blowing back towards the Earth's stern or downstream side. This interaction causes what's referred to as a magnetic explosion. Some of the Earth's own magnetic energy is suddenly converted to heat and kinetic energy that sends massive amounts of charged particles streaming down along our magnetic field lines. This sudden transfer of energy sparks brilliant auroras that are visible into the Deep South, reaching almost to Mexico. It can also damage GPS and radio communications satellites. The repair after a sudden break is called magnetic reconnection.[7]

The continuous aurora oval is caused by electron "leakage" flowing around Earth's magnetic fields, but this low-energy aurora isn't conspicuous from the ground. We use satellites to continuously monitor this energy flow, but these cameras typically record in the ultraviolet spectrum to reduce the effects of blue light scattering.[8]

Find the Northern Dancers

Other planets with sufficient gravity and atmosphere also feature auroras, including Jupiter and Saturn. But you'll probably have better luck catching the northern lights over Glacier National Park. Most of the park's valleys run east-west, while most of our auroras hug the north horizon. The Waterton Valley runs north, so Goat Haunt is a good place to watch from, as is Big Prairie in the North Fork. But probably the best location is also the most convenient — the Apgar beach along Lake McDonald's south shore. Be sure to check out the aurora web services listed in the *Resources* section. The lights aren't too hard to see, even in summer. But hurry — the magnetic north pole is moving away from us at about 25 miles (40 km) per year.

"Pleiades and Northern Lights." *Curtains of northern lights dance and sway over Kintla Lake shortly after midnight, while the Pleiades watches from a notch between the mountains just above the northeastern horizon.*

"Great Northern Lights" (this page). The aurora borealis reflects on the surface of Waterton Lake, framing the Prince of Wales Hotel which was completed in 1927 by the Great Northern Railroad. On this night, the northern lights were caused by a rare wrinkle in the Earth's gravitational field. I was on location to photograph the Milky Way on a clear, moonless night when a green glow suddenly appeared.

"Midnight Symphony" (facing page). Northern lights dance and sway across a Lake McDonald dance floor in April 2003. All three images were made on the same night, less than 30 minutes apart. These northern lights were caused by a blast of solar radiation, so I knew there was a good chance for them to appear on schedule. A yellow band appeared at about 11:30 p.m., and the colors started dancing just after midnight.

"Milky Way Aurora" *(above).*
The bright, summer Milky Way
arcs into a lavender, northern sky.

"Moonlit Aurora" *(upper right).*
Pillars of color reach for the sky
above the North Fork Valley
on a moonlit night. The moon
doesn't affect northern lights,
but moonlight often overpowers
the aurora.

"Green Skies" *(near right).*
Curtains of green northern lights
pulsate over Lake McDonald.

AIR GLOW AURORA

Imagine a cloud rainbow so long and thin that it wraps all the way around the planet. That's sort of what air glow look might look like, if only we could see it. Layers of red, green, yellow and blue circle the Earth, but they're too faint to register on our color-detecting cone cells. Air glow is brightest during the day because it's a sun-driven phenomenon. Nighttime air glow is just 1/1000ths as bright and is mostly found in photographs of the darkest skies.[1]

While northern lights result from occasional gusts of solar wind (high-speed electrons and protons), air glow is caused by the sun's gentle breeze (ultraviolet light) that you don't notice. Both are classified as auroras and occur at similar altitudes. At Glacier's location, the northern lights tend to stick close to our northern horizon, but they can also show up high in the night sky. Air glow is so dim that it's mosty detected about 10–15 degrees above the horizon in any direction, where you're peering through lots of atmosphere.

On our sunlit side, air glow occurs where solar waves crash into the Earth's gravity waves, and atmospheric molecules get caught in the melee. Incoming infrared radiation charges up electrons in atoms and molecules of oxygen, nitrogen and sodium. A chemical-reaction glow, called "chemoluminescence," results from the vibrations and crashes among the formerly-invisible particles.

Instead of vertical sheets, air glow forms distinct layers at different altitudes, like thin clouds. Red forms a thick layer at 90–185 miles (150–300 km) altitude, where excited hydroxyl radicals (-OH) react with atoms of oxygen and nitrogen. The brightest color, green, forms at 56–62 miles (90–100 km), where charged-up oxygen and nitrogen atoms collide. Below this, weak blue air glow appears at 59 miles (95 km) from excited oxygen molecules (O_2).[2]

The most intriguing air glow lives between the red and green layers, at an altitude of 57 miles (92 km). Yellow air glow results from infrared radiation striking sodium atoms. We used to think this sodium originated from rising vapors of evaporated sea water. Instead, analysis now shows that *meteors* deliver this sodium to our atmosphere.[3]

"Mount Reynolds Milky Way." *A shooting star falls from the Milky Way above Mount Reynolds, near Logan Pass. Horizontal clouds of green and red air glow are visible in the lower third of the sky. Air glow is an electrical-chemical phenomenon that's always present in the upper atmosphere, but it's only visible in the darkest settings. It's a reaction between solar radiation, Earth's weak gravity and thin atmosphere. If you look closely at the other moonless images in this book, you can find air glow aurora in most of them.*

MILKY WAY GALAXY ~ THE WOLF'S TRAIL

The ancient Greeks called it *Galaxias kuklos*, the "Milky Circle." The Romans knew it as *Via lactea*, the "Milky Way." Traditional Blackfoot see it differently. They call it *Makoyohsokoyi*, the "Wolf's Trail."[1] When people die, according to the Blackfoot story, their spirits travel along the Wolf's Trail to the Sky World, where their campfires sparkle once again at night like so many stars. Smoke from their fires form the dark areas. Every clear night is an opportunity to look up and remember family and friends who have journeyed on ahead of us.[2]

The Milky Way is still growing. Gas and dust clouds give birth to about 20 new stars each year. It also captures millions of stars from smaller galaxies with its far-reaching gravity. During its 12-billion-year lifetime, the Milky Way has absorbed at least six entire galaxies. It's currently peeling stars away from the nearby Sagittarius Dwarf galaxy.[3]

A handsome neighbor, the Andromeda galaxy, is even bigger than the Milky Way. In a marriage made in the heavens, these two galaxies are heading towards a blind date in two billion years.[4] They'll swirl around each other in an ever-tightening spiral until the two become one. Our sun will be there as a bridesmaid, but you and I needn't worry about wedding gifts.

When you're driving cross-country on your way to somewhere, you won't pass by here. Glacier National Park really isn't on the way to anywhere else. You have to go out of your way, driving on two-lane roads for hours to get lost in this part of Montana. That, and our impressive collection of potholes are two reasons why we can still see the Milky Way from here. The ability to see the Milky Way on clear, moonless nights has become the litmus test to measure how much light pollution surrounds you. On the Bortle scale of 1 to 9, where 1 is comparable to pre-industrial darkness, most of the park is now between 1 and 2.

When you stare at the night sky from a place that's dark enough to reveal the Milky Way, what you see in real time is actually ancient history. The sunlight you see during the day is 8.3 minutes old. But when you look at the Milky Way's next-closest star, Alpha Centauri, your eye is catching light that was hurled in our direction 4.22 years ago — and that's traveling at light speed. If you flew to this star at space shuttle speed, the trip would take 165,000 Earth years, not including pit stops.[5]

All of the sparkling fires in our Milky Way arrive together from different points in the past. When you find yourself getting to Sirius, the brightest star in the Milky Way, you're seeing light that left there 8.6 years ago. Our pole star, Polaris, points the way north with light that's 323 years old. The star in Orion's right shoulder, Betelgeuse, is just now updating you on what happened there 643 years ago.[6] This red super-giant is due to explode soon, in an astronomical timescale. It could have gone supernovae 543 years ago and we wouldn't find out for another century. It always takes a little longer for news to reach Montana.

If you stare in awe of the Milky Way long enough, you'll start to notice another little-known tidbit. Most of the stars in our night sky are colorful, not white.[7] Our eyes can only detect the stars' true colors when we view them from the darkest places. Remember Alpha Centauri? It's actually a cluster of three red stars. Polaris is a yellow super-giant double star, and Betelgeuse is still a red super-giant — at least, as far as we know.

Colorful and faint stars are the first things lost to artificial light. Is an orange, luminous fog truly more valuable to our civilization than the vision of sparkling ancestral campfires along the Wolf's Trail?

Remember the Wolf's Trail

The Milky Way is most impressive on clear and moonless nights between June and August. That's when we're looking in towards our galaxy's star-studded center. We look out at a thinly-populated region of the Milky Way during the rest of the year. Two of my favorite viewing locations are Logan Pass and the Wild Goose Island overlook. You won't see much until your eyes have adapted to darkness for 20 to 30 minutes. Close them and listen for wolves howling.

"Chief Mountain Cloudy Milky Way" (left). Chief Mountain watches the Milky Way as it passes overhead just after midnight. The orange glow in the clouds is from outdoor "safety" lights in Babb.

"Rock Stars" (facing page). A late-summer Milky Way glows above the stones in Two Medicine Lake.

"Midnight Train" (below). The Wolf's Trail Milky Way sparkles above Mount Saint Nicholas, while the headlight from a midnight train shines across the lower foothills.

"Waterton Valley Milky Way." *The spring Milky Way falls into Goat Haunt, near the northern edge of Glacier National Park and the southern end of Waterton Lake. Light from Waterton town site forms a glow that hides some of the Milky Way's fainter stars. And if you look carefully at the snowy mountaintops, you can also see a green cast that is from a display of northern lights (page 25) in the sky behind the camera. At one point in time, the lake we currently know as Waterton was briefly, and mistakenly, named Chief Mountain Lake.*[8]

These three Glacier National Park images illustrate how dust and twilight can affect how the stars look in the Milky Way. **"Wild Goose Milky Way"** (left) was made in the summer, when we tend to have more dust or smoke in the air. Can you spot the planet among the stars? **"Chief Mountain Milky Way"** (center) was made during an early summer, moonless night. Total darkness stretched the capabilities of that particular camera sensor. And **"Heavens Above"** (right) shows Heavens Peak and was made about two hours closer to twilight than the other images. This slight change in timing was enough for the sky to start coming back to scattered blue. If you look closely at all three images, you can also see faint magenta and green clouds of horizontal air glow (page 27).

TRAILS ACROSS THE SKY

'd like to pause our tour here for a moment to eat a little bit of trail mix and describe a little bit of photography. Specifically, I feel the need to explain star trail images like these.

A camera is just a light-proof box with some kind of light-sensitive something-or-other inside. We started with wet gel, moved on to film, and now we have fancy digital sensors hidden in there — but the concept remains the same. Uncover the camera's opening (lens) in the dark, and nothing happens inside. But when there's enough light

on the outside, magic starts happening on the sensor. The stars are recorded as tiny points of light, only one pixel across unless you forget to focus the lens (yes, it happens).

If you're lucky, it's still good and dark at night where you live. Mount a camera onto a tripod in the dark, point it at the stars, and lock the shutter open. Find a comfortable seat, watch for shooting stars, take a nap, and expose the image for a good hour or more. Actually, nowadays we most commonly stack lots of consecutive 30-second

images together. A 10-hour winter night can yield 1,200 frames to combine into one final image.

While the Earth slowly rotates around its north-south axis, the stars appear to slowly move in a big circle around Polaris, the North Star. Our brains can't detect it in real time, but the camera can. Expose the shadow box for more than an hour, and the result is a photograph of circular star trails in the night sky. They're real photographs of real events that really happen. But to me, star trail images are still a bit magical.

"Mount Brown Fire Lookout" (above). A series of 30-second exposures are edited to turn the star trails into fireballs flying past the fire lookout on Mount Brown.

"Stars and Stones" (right). This 45-minute star trails image over Lake McDonald combines three camera techniques. I "painted" on the rocks with a flashlight during a long exposure, and the crescent moon is a standard, short exposure. Both elements were captured in place, in-camera. You can see a glow on the horizon from the town of Cardston, and a small glow above Lake McDonald Lodge.

"Two Medicine Star Trails." *Combining a few hours of consecutive photographs into one image shows the stars' apparent movement across the night sky above Two Medicine Lake. In this west-facing scene, there are a few breaks in the star trails from scattered clouds, and the reflected red lights of a passing plane. The orange-brown glow on the horizon is from the lights of the Flathead Valley.*

"Ancient Circles." *The night sky appears to revolve around Polaris, the North Star, in this north-facing time-lapse image. But it's really the Earth that is rotating in this view of the sky from the Lake McDonald shoreline near Sprague Creek. Lake McDonald is a sacred area to the traditional Kootenai. For generations, the tribe gathered each spring on the shores of Lake McDonald for the Bear Dance Ceremony. The original Kootenai name for the lake is* Yakilhaqwilnamki, *which translates into, "Where (people) dance." The Blackfeet name for this lake is* Kyaiyo-Ahtiwapixi, *or "The Bear Wags its Tail."*[1]

POLARIS ~ THE STAR THAT STANDS STILL

Traditional Blackfoot know Polaris as *Apatohsi-Kakatosi*,[2] "The Star That Stands Still."[3] The tiny point of light that we call the North Star is only the 49th-brightest star in the night sky, but Polaris is famous for other reasons. There's a lot more to the North Star than meets the eye.

As Earth spins, an imaginary line starting from the South Pole and continuing through the North Pole points to Polaris in the nighttime sky. Because of its prime parking spot, Polaris appears to stay put while all the other stars appear to circle around it.

Polaris is the last star in the Little Dipper's handle, but you need good, dark skies to see this constellation (Ursa Minor). It's directly over your fur-lined tuque if you're standing on the North Pole. When you hang around Glacier National Park, which dangles from the 49th parallel, Polaris sits roughly 49 degrees above the horizon (if you could find a level horizon). Wherever you live in the northern hemisphere, the latitude of your town is also the North Star's height above your horizon, in degrees.

Back in the 1780s, German-born William Herschel peered through a telescope at Polaris and discovered that it has a companion star. More recently, we learned that Polaris is a multiple star system comprised of one super-giant (the star we see) with two small companion stars and two more distant components. As stars go, one of the small companions orbits the super-giant very closely, about the same distance as from our sun to Uranus.

The Polaris super-giant is also our closest variable star, or Cepheid. Variable stars expand and contract during very precise and distinct pulsations periods. A Cepheid's diameter increases by millions of miles while it flashes brightly for a few days or months (depending on the star). Then it collapses back into its smaller, darker self.

But maybe the most surprising thing about Polaris is that the job it's famous for is just a temporary gig. It'll be the North Star for the duration of your life (for hundreds of generations, actually), but Polaris will only serve as Earth's pole star for about 4,000 years. It's been in a usable position since around 800 AD, and it's still on a super-slow-motion approach. Polaris is currently about 0.7 degrees from the north axis. Its gig as the North Star will peak on March 24, 2100, when it will occupy the night sky less than half a degree from true north.[4]

Polaris certainly "stands still" in human time. But its apparent location is continuously changing, albeit very slowly. Why? Because the Earth is wobbly, and our north-south axis makes a great big circle across the sky every 25,765 years.[5] This is called the Earth's precession.

Imagine a child's toy, a top with a pencil sticking straight up out of the center. Spin the top, hold a piece of paper level above it, and the pencil draws a circle. Against a fixed backdrop of stars, the Earth's precession makes a slow circle that passes a handful of visible stars, like Polaris, and a whole bunch of empty space. This was first discovered sometime around 130 BC by Hipparchus, a Greek astronomer plying his trade 1,700 years before telescopes were invented.[6]

Sediments that would become what we know as Chief Mountain were laid down 1,500 million years ago.[7] Since then, the Earth has made more than 58,200 precessional laps. We don't yet know the age of Polaris. But we do know that Glacier's rocks are older than some of the other part-time pole stars.

We can tour the northern sky both backwards and forwards in time to discover different pole stars. Five thousand years ago the Egyptians used the North Star of their time, Thuban, when designing their famous pyramids.[8] (Thuban is only one-quarter as bright as Polaris, lost from our view now in urban areas due to light pollution.) Thuban is 550 million years old, much younger than Chief Mountain.[9]

A closer and brighter star, Vega, was the pole star about 14,000 years ago, and it will return to the pole position in the year 13,727 AD. After our sun, Vega was the first star to ever be photographed and have its spectrum measured (visible, x-ray and radio). Vega's about 500 million years old.[10]

Closer to home, when you find Polaris from your campsite in Glacier National Park, it is currently located one degree east (left) of north, and one degree above north. Polaris was two degrees east of north when the park was officially designated in 1910. So in this span of time, Polaris appears to have moved about the width of two full moons, as seen from your campsite. (The full moon appears about 0.5 degrees wide in the sky.)[11]

Polaris was two degrees further east (four full moons), and one degree above north when the park's current glaciers were at their peak size (about 1845 AD). When the current glaciers first formed (roughly 5,000 BC), Polaris was nowhere near the Earth's north axis. Back then it was 42 degrees further east, and 16 degrees lower. Empty space occupied Earth's pole position.[12]

The older, more massive glaciers that carved the park's valleys and revealed its mountain peaks were actually from a different round of glaciation, about 10,000 years ago. You wouldn't need a campsite reservation, but you'd need to bring your own wood for the campfire. Back then Polaris would have been 49 degrees further east and 26 degrees lower than its current position.[13]

Point Out the (Current) North Star

Polaris shines brightly in Glacier's night sky, but there have been a few times when I just couldn't find it. Each time, it slowly dawned on me that Polaris was hiding behind a mountain.

Polaris is easy to find if you have a clear view to the north. First, locate the Big Dipper. The dipper's front two stars are called pointer stars. If you connect them with an imaginary line, and then extend this line above the dipper for about five lengths, you'll find yourself at Polaris.

BIG DIPPER ~ SEVEN BROTHERS IN THE GREAT BEAR

The most familiar stars in our entire night sky is a family of seven lights that we call the "Big Dipper." They belong to the third-largest constellation, Ursa Major, the "Great Bear." The Big Dipper's brightest stars are still visible from towns with moderate amounts of light pollution, but the Great Bear appears to have vanished from the night skies over our cities. These seven stars serve as compass, clock and calendar.

The Big Dipper's stars are the seven sons of Sun and Moon[1] in one Blackfoot story. Another traditional story calls them *Ihkitsikammiksi*, the Seven Brothers in the Great Bear.[2] Blackfeet often paint the Seven Brothers on a tepee's north smoke flap, sometimes depicted as a seven-star crescent moon.[3,4,5]

The story of the Seven Brothers[6,7,8] tells of a small Blackfoot camp that included a family of seven sons and two daughters. After the six oldest sons left camp to go on a long hunting trip, the oldest sister fell in love with a bear, whom she married. When her parents found out, they became angry and the whole camp surrounded the bear and killed him. The enraged daughter used her dead husband's medicine to turn into a huge bear, and then she killed everyone in camp except for her little brother and sister. She returned to human form and plotted how to kill her six brothers as soon as they returned. But her young brother and sister slipped away in the night and warned the returning hunters. They all fled but soon found the angry bear fast on their heels.

When they came upon a tall tree, the seven brothers and their little sister climbed into the branches. The great bear was able to knock down her little sister and three of her brothers, and was about to kill them, when the youngest brother shot a medicine arrow into the air. His little sister immediately left for the sky. He shot six more arrows skyward, and then he joined his six brothers and little sister as a family of stars.

The Seven Brothers take the same positions in the sky that they took in the tree branches. If you look closely at the center star of the bear's tail

(the dipper's handle), you will see that there is a little star right next to it. That star is little sister. Astronomers know her as Alcor.

As for the Great Bear having a long tail, there are stories for that as well. For the ancient Greeks, Zeus saved the Great Bear — and her cub, Ursa Minor — from death by grabbing their tails and swinging them overhead and throwing both into the sky.[9] A Roman story has Jupiter reaching down and lifting these bears into the sky by their tails. Their tails just got stretched a little.[10] Instead of a long tail, some North American tribes see three hunters following a short-tailed bear, and the hunter in the middle is carrying a cooking pot.[11]

The Seven Brothers or Big Dipper can be seen from two-thirds of the Earth, but it's especially noticeable from the Northern Hemisphere. Viewed from Glacier, the Brothers spend all night circling the North Star counter-clockwise and never set below the horizon (unless, of course, you're standing on the south face of a steep mountain). The two brothers in the farthest tree branch point out the north star. Draw a line between them and extend this by five lengths, and that's where you'll find Polaris. Once you know north, then you know all four directions.

Find Polaris and you'll also find the Great Bear's cub. The north star is the last one in the handle of Ursa Minor, the Little Bear. But the cub's stars are not nearly as bright as those in the Great Bear, and they can be hard to see even in the dark skies above Glacier.

In addition to a handy compass, the Great Bear's stars also serve as a clock and calendar. Like a big hour hand in the sky, you can imagine the handle pointing out 12 divisions for hours. The handle revolves once every 23 hours and 56 minutes. If the handle points down at 9 p.m., then you know that in one-quarter of a revolution the handle will point right or east six hours later, at 3 a.m. when you wake in your sleeping bag. You only have to look up and see where little brother is pointing.[12]

The Great Bear's tail also marks the four seasons.[13] At 9 p.m. the tail/handle points up in summer, left/west in fall, down in winter, and right/east in spring. One way to remember this is to think of the tail as an icicle hanging down in winter and as grass growing up in summer.

Spot Little Sister

All Seven Brothers in the Big Dipper are about the same brightness, and they stand out from neighboring stars. But Alcor, their little sister, can be hard to distinguish from her nearby brother. If you have trouble spotting her at first, using a pair of binoculars should help bring her nicely into view.

"Seven Brothers in Winter" (left). The Seven Brothers point down towards a moonlit Mount Cannon in winter. If you look closely at the middle of the handle, you can see little sister next to her brother.

"Sign of Winter" (facing page). If snow and below-zero air temperatures aren't enough to signal winter, then you can count on the Big Dipper's handle pointing down at midnight to tell you.

"Big Dipper in Summer" (below). At midnight in the summer, the Big Dipper's handle points left or west.

ORION IN THE SKY

The Big Dipper is the most familiar star pattern in our sky, but isn't a constellation. It's an asterism, a star pattern within a larger group that we call Ursa Major, which really is a constellation. In 1930 the International Astronomical Union divided the night sky into 88 official regions, sort of like counties, that are the official constellations.[3] So the term "constellation" can refer to a group of stars or to a region of sky. Confusing, yes?

Orion the hunter is easily the most recognizable constellation. It's visible from around the world and has spawned stories throughout recorded history. The ancient Greeks gave it the Orion name, but older Arabic illustrations showed this constellation as a woman hunter named *al-Jauza*. There must have been something in the air, however, because in later illustrations the name changed to *al-Jabar*, a masculine word for giant.[4]

Arabic astronomers named the giant's right shoulder star, *yad al-jauza*. But Arabic y and b characters look similar, and European scholars who transcribed Arabic history centuries later misread the Arabic name and Latinized it as *bedelgeuze,* which is pretty close to the name that we currently use, Betelgeuse.[5,6]

Some of Orion's feminine history remains in the Arabic name used for his/her left shoulder star, Bellatrix, which means "female warrior." Orion's remaining corner stars are named Rigel ("left foot of the central one") and Saiph ("sword").[7]

Betelgeuse and Rigel are among the 10 brightest in the night sky, and all but one of Orion's stars (Bellatrix) belong to family lines that travel together. These are all relatively young stars, as this region is home to dense clouds of dust and gas that are super star nurseries. More than 10,000 young stars have formed in this region so far, but most are well below naked-eye visibility. Orion's brightest stars started popping up 12 million years ago, when the expanding shock waves from distant supernova explosions started rocking these dust clouds.[8] All of Orion's stars

except for Bellatrix will explode into supernovas while still relatively young. Betelgeuse will be the first to go, glowing as bright as the full moon. This supernova will be visible even in the daytime for a few weeks or months.[9] These explosions will mean the end of Orion, but they will also spark new rounds of star formation in the same region. Maybe Orion's demise will create a new constellation, and maybe next time around she will return to her former, female form.

Betelgeuse also demonstrates one of the dictums of astronomy — stars twinkle often, while planets only twinkle when they're near the horizon. Seen from earth, most lights from space twinkle at night because you're looking through the thin ocean of atmosphere that surrounds us. The air is in constant motion, and its density is constantly changing. The motion and density fluxuations bend the incoming light, especially near the horizon where you are looking through the most atmosphere.[10] The crux of the twinkling difference is that stars (other than the sun) are so far from us that they appear as tiny points of self-illuminating light. On the other hand, planets are relatively close by, so they are comparatively wide sources of reflected light. The light we see from a

planet is also bent by our atmosphere, but it tends to get smoothed out by additional light reflecting from the rest of the disk.[11] As point sources of light, starlight dances like no one's watching.

Betelgeuse is Orion's brightest star, and its dance card fits somewhere between placid planet and dancing with the stars. It's 500 times larger and 16,000 times brighter than our sun, but its surface temperature is roughly one-half that of the sun. It's relatively close by as stars go, just 430 light years away. With this combination of characteristics, Betelgeuse is a bright point of light when viewed with the naked eye, but it becomes a planet-like disk of light when viewed through a good telescope. So Betelgeuse dances while you're just looking around the neighborhood, but it stands still if you zoom in and stare.

Track the Hunter

Orion the Hunter is winter's vibrant constellation. It rises at sunset starting around the first of the year, and moves due south at sunset by early March. In mid-May, however, Orion begins to slip below the horizon just as it becomes visible in the evening twilight.

"Orion the Hunter" *(left). Orion trips over Singleshot Mountain while crossing the sky on a winter night. The constellation's highest star, Betelgeuse (upper left), reflects from shallows of the Saint Mary River. A moonless night sky should be dark blue or black, but this sky is reflecting the orange, electric lights of Saint Mary. Singleshot Mountain was named by a hunting party. James Willard Schultz provided the name in 1887 after George Bird Grinnell brought down a running mountain goat with a single shot from his heavy Sharps rifle, 150 yards away in a snowstorm.*[1,2]

"Orion's Companions" *(facing page). Orion graces the midnight sky above Chief Mountain. The hunter is accompanied by our largest planet, Jupiter (middle right), and our brightest star, Sirius (lower left). Seen from the Chief Mountain overlook, lights from the Flathead Valley, 55 air miles away, color the sky above Yellow Mountain.*

"Orionid Meteor" *(below). A fast Orionid meteor leaves a short trail near Betelgeuse, the red giant star that is Orion's right shoulder, as the constellation rises behind clouds above the Livingston mountain range. The night lights of West Glacier also glow orange in the clouds.*

PLEIADES ~ THE LOST BOYS

When you stare into Glacier's dark skies, maybe hoping to catch a "falling star," there are lots of standing stars that might just catch your fancy. The Big Dipper is the most familiar group, and Orion the Hunter really stands out during winter. But there is a smaller, fainter cluster that appears to be the favorite of many cultures — including the Japanese, who know it as *Subaru* (just look at the car company's logo).

There are many stories related to the star cluster that you and I now know as the Pleiades. The traditional Blackfoot name is *Miohpoisiks*, the "Bunched Stars."[1] Their story is unusual because, while most cultures see the Pleiades as six or seven young girls or sisters, the Blackfoot see them as six little boys, often brothers.[2]

The brothers belonged to the poorest family in camp. Their father wasn't a good hunter, and their mother only managed to collect a few berries and roots to eat. All of the other kids wore the yellow robes from buffalo calves, which were born in springtime. They teased the brothers about their worn-out, brown robes, and the other adults were sometimes mean to the boys as well. So the boys decided to go away to a place where they would not be mistreated, and they climbed into the sky where the Moon took good care of them.

The brothers asked the Moon to punish the people for their bad behavior, and the Moon convinced her husband the Sun to stop the rain. Blackfoot country got very hot, and the rivers and lakes dried up. The camp dogs dug into the riverbanks to make the first springs, but these dried up as well. After six days, the Dog Chief prayed to the Sun and told him that all of the animals were suffering. The rain returned, and now the dogs sometimes howl at the sky because they miss the lost boys.[3,4]

Retold over generations of crackling campfires, this Blackfoot story reminds parents to treat all children well, not just their own.

Blackfeet often painted six stars on one of their tepee smoke flaps, including several tepees that were photographed in the park after Glacier had been officially dedicated.[5,6] I'm especially partial to this story because of my own upbringing. I come from a hardscrabble family of seven sons, not six. And these days our dogs miss me terribly when I spend all night out photographing under Glacier's stars.

The Blackfoot story tells of six boys, but up to 14 stars are naked-eye visible in the Pleiades, depending on your vision and the quality of your darkness. Using any old pair of binoculars in a dark, park campground reveals dozens of stars in the cluster. A telescope reveals hundreds more that, like brothers or sisters, are all related.

The Pleiades family includes more than 1,000 hungry young stars, siblings born from a single cloud of dust and gas. The trajectory of this cloud traces back to a single exploding star about 100 million years ago. It's currently surrounded by an unrelated nebula, a beautiful blue cloud that the cluster is moving through. The Pleiades' brightest stars shine through the dust and illuminate this cloud.[7] It looks blue to us because of light scattering, the same phenomenon that makes our own sunlit sky look blue.

From our earthly viewpoint, the Pleiades occupies about four moon widths, or 2 degrees. The cluster looks small and faint from here, but we've found that the individual stars are actually 40 to 2,400 times brighter than our sun.[8]

Find the Lost Boys

Where Montana lies in the northern hemisphere, the "Bunched Stars" are visible all night long during November. You can see them in the evening sky from October to April, and in the morning sky from late June to December. But when the buffalo are calving in May and early June, the six brothers join the Sun so that they can't be seen.

"Moon Joins the Stars." A full moon peers over the Livingston Range in Glacier's North Fork Valley. Moonlight washes out the Milky Way, but the Pleiades (middle right) and the Andromeda galaxy (upper right) are still clearly visible.

"Pleiades Setting." *The Pleiades constellation sets over Singleshot Mountain in Glacier's Saint Mary Valley. In this cluster of young stars, six are naked-eye visible, more than a dozen are seen through a telephoto lens (above), and hundreds are revealed by a telescope. Lights from Saint Mary cast a faint, orange glow onto the snow.*

Some comets don't play by the rules. For this reason many cultures around the world came to regard comets as bad omens, and a broom star's unexpected arrival brought more fear than wonder. For traditional Blackfeet, the appearance of a "star-feeding" is taken as a sign that sickness and starvation will arrive the following winter.[1]

On January 27, 1910, a page-one headline from the *Choteau Acantha* newspaper announced "An Unexpected Comet." From Montana, the first comet of 1910 was easily visible for over a month, between sunset and 9 p.m.[2] No one person was credited with its discovery, so it was simply named the Great Comet due to its long tail.[3]

A few months later, Glacier National Park was officially dedicated on May 11. When it was just eight days old, the park (along with the rest of Earth) passed through a dusty trail from the most famous comet of all, the one named for British astronomer Edmund Halley. Halley's comet is a celestial snowball that gets flung past us every 74 to 79 years, last gracing Glacier's skies in 1986.

Halley's was the only comet to show up on the historical Plains Indian calendars, the winter counts. The 1910 return was recorded by at least six different Blackfoot bands, including one count belonging to the Pikuni Blackfeet.[4]

Most comets are not quite as famous. The average comet is about six miles (10 km) in diameter, too small to generate much gravity, so they tend to form lumpy potato shapes instead of spheres.[5]

Comets are just dark, dusty snowballs until they approach the sun. The nucleus consists of mostly frozen carbon dioxide, water ice, rocks and space dust. Solar radiation turns the ice directly into vapor ("sublimates") and plasma that form a dense cloud, or coma, around the nucleus. Dust particles blown out by escaping gases leave a visible dust tail up to 6 million miles (10 million km) long. Plasma from the coma gets blown away by the solar wind and forms a second, faint-blue ion tail. The glowing nucleus and coma also

create a hydrogen cloud that's millions of miles in diameter, but we can't see this with our eyes.[6]

Most comets spend their time hidden from view. The only time we see them is when their elliptical orbits pull them in close to the sun, which then flings them back out into space. We classify comets as short-period (Jupiter-type), medium-period (Halley-type) or long-period.

Short-period comets are frequent and familiar visitors that make the round trip in less than 20 years. The most frequent comet shows up every 3.2 years. These comets originate in the Kuiper Belt, out beyond the orbit of Neptune. Icy bodies in this doughnut-shaped belt orbit the sun in circular paths along the same plane as the planets. When gravity disturbs one of these snowballs, it falls into an elliptical orbit and becomes a comet.[7]

The best-known comet, Halley's, is a medium-period comet. These have orbits between 20 and 200 years. Medium-period and long-period comets originate even further out, in the spherical Oort cloud. While all of our planets and asteroids circle the sun in roughly the same plane, the Oort cloud forms a globe around our solar system. It extends

halfway out to the next nearest star. We can't see them that far away, but the evidence points to more than one billion chunks of ice and rock circling the sun in round orbits.[8]

Every now and then, an Oort cloud body gets pushed by light or pulled by dust clouds. This little nudge causes it to fall towards the sun on a long, elliptical orbit. Long-period comets have orbits between 200 and 2000 years.[9]

Roughly 70,000 years ago, a pair of dwarf stars passed through the Oort cloud without tossing any snowballs at Earth.[10] But Oort cloud ejections are the comets that were most responsible for terrorizing so many cultures. After moving into an elliptical orbit, they might have appeared only once in recorded history. They also come in from all directions, and their arrival is always a surprise. That's just too scary for many people.[11]

The most impressive comet ever witnessed, hands down, was Shoemaker-Levy IX. It was discovered in March 1993 orbiting Jupiter instead of the sun. Astronomers calculated that the massive planet's gravity must have snatched this comet from its elliptical orbit about 20 years earlier. Jupiter's gravity broke the comet into nine pieces that plunged into the gas planet's clouds, leaving swirling eddies that were visible for months. We saw firsthand how Jupiter protects our little blue planet by eating comets.[12]

The European Space Agency recently placed a satellite into orbit around a comet (67P) and landed a probe on its surface.[13] Soon, we should understand comets much better and maybe feel a little more wonder when they visit.

Mountain Comets

Have no fear, you can go comet-watching in Glacier. But it requires a little homework and lots of warm clothes. Comet orbits and locations are widely available on websites and desktop planetariums, like Stellarium (see *Resources*). But for most comets you'll still need binoculars or a telescope. Plus warm gloves and thick socks.

"Comet Among Star Trails" *(above). Comet Panstarrs (C/2011 L4) swings past Mount Stanton and Mount Vaught in April 2013.*

"Moonlit Comet" *(near left). Comet Lovejoy of 2013 (C/2013 R1) shows a visible tail in spite of 87% moon illumination on Mount Cannon.*

"Lovejoy" *(this page far left). Comet Lovejoy of 2013 (C/2013 R1) rises above Mount Brown on a moonless night in December 2013.*

"Clouded Comet" *(facing page). Comet Lovejoy of 2014 (C/2014 Q2) fades into thin clouds on the horizon above Chief Mountain.*

"Lovejoy Lookout." *On a -10F/-23C December night in 2014, Comet Lovejoy (C/2014 Q2) sets behind the fire lookout on Huckleberry Mountain. The 66.7% moon illumination lights up the snow-covered slopes, but it also washes out the comet's twin tails.*

"Silent Night." On a -11F/-24C December night in 2013, Comet Lovejoy (C/2013 R1) rises over Mount Brown (right) while the winter Milky Way dives into Mount Stanton (left). This Comet Lovejoy will visit us every 14,011 years. The bright star Vega casts its reflection on the lake from its position close to the horizon. Vega was our north star about 14,000 years ago, and it will return to the pole position in the year 13,727 AD. I waited many months for a chance to make this image. When a rare, clear winter night finally arrived in December, the lake was fogged over and I couldn't see the sky. I waited four hours before the fog parted long enough for me to photograph this tranquil scene.

"Leonid Meteor Over the North Fork River." *A Leonid meteor flares over a bend in the North Fork of the Flathead River in early December 2014. The annual Leonid meteor shower lasts for about six weeks, peaking in late November. The Leonid shower of 1833 is still considered the most spectacular shower in recorded history, with upwards of 240,000 meteors per hour lighting up northwestern skies for nine hours. The trail of space dust responsible for the Leonid meteor showers is refreshed every 33 years by comet 55P/Tempel-Tuttle.*

WHEN STARS FALL

By all accounts, the Leonid meteor storm of 1833 was one of the most spectacular sights in recorded history. On the night of November 12–13, people in the northern Rockies reported more than 200,000 meteors per hour for nine hours. More than a storm, this was a meteor blizzard. This sky event showed up in every one of the Plains Indian winter counts, including those from four different Blackfoot groups. One of these glyphs was transcribed as "Winter when the stars fell."[1]

In 1929, two Flathead-Kalispel historians shared a sky story with a white historian living in Ronan.[2] They spoke of a flaming star that dove into Flathead Lake, a meteor story they said was passed down from long-ago generations. It started long after dark, when a loud shriek overhead brought everyone out of their warm tepees. A flaming star as bright as the sun screamed past them and dove into the lake near Wild Horse Island. A steam cloud formed above the waves. Several brave but frightened men paddled out in their canoes and found warm waters, with many cooked fish floating on the surface.

"Heavenly Visitor Makes Polson." This page-one headline in *The Flathead Courier* announced another meteor strike on September 1, 1911. "*Those who observed the heavenly visitor say it was a sight long to be remembered and resembled a skyrocket the size of a barrel.*" This meteor also appeared to dive into Flathead Lake.[3]

Another meteor toured Montana without stopping on August 10, 1972. This was an "Earth grazer" fireball, seen easily in daylight, and moving very slowly for a meteor. While it casually cruised to the northwest across more than 900 miles (1,450 km) of big sky, camera-toting tourists in Grand Teton, Yellowstone and Glacier National Parks watched the meteor for at least 100 seconds. It skipped off the atmosphere and headed back into space, and some of Glacier's camera-toting visitors headed back home with a photo souvenir.[4]

Just like us, stars begin to die the moment they are born. And each dying star contributes to the birth of the next generation of stars. Every element beyond basic hydrogen is created (fused) in the nuclear heart of a star. Each star birth and supernova death flings debris and gases in all directions: iron, nickel, calcium, gold, oxygen, helium, carbon dioxide. Clouds of gaseous debris expelled by the sun's birth formed our distant gas giants — Jupiter, Saturn, Uranus and Neptune. The rocky, inner debris left behind swirled into a primordial belt, colliding and clumping into proto-planets that became Mercury, Venus, Earth, and Mars. Young planets endured heavy bombardments from meteorites, comets and asteroids while also sweeping their orbits clear of space debris.[5,6]

Leftover construction debris still remains in parts of our solar system. Rounding the sun between the orbits of Jupiter and Mars is a spacious belt of about 1–2 million rocky asteroids and one "dwarf planet" (Ceres). Jupiter's crushing gravity keeps this debris from clumping together into a planet.[7,8]

It took a long time for our raucous teenage planet to settle down. Major collisions tapered off and Earth's crust cooled. Once a solid surface formed, the water and amino acids delivered daily by asteroids stayed put instead of vaporizing into space.[9,10,11] The ingredients necessary for life were coming together in this big melting pot planet, delivered by various forms of star dust. Our planet still rams into countless asteroids every day, but the vast majority are micro-meteorites.

Our atmosphere doesn't slow down the biggest asteroids much, and they come in fast. But the vast majority of "shooting stars" are caused by specks the size of a sand grain. Slamming in at speeds up to 162,000 mph (257,500 km/hr), ram pressure heats air molecules into a glow that we can see.[12] Some meteors leave a smoke trail that can last for many minutes. The fastest meteors also create brief aurora trails that are faint but measurable.[13]

The Earth catches an estimated 100 tons of space debris every day. Our daily delivery amounts to roughly 100 billion micro-meteorites (the diameter of a human hair), 25 million specks the size of a sand grain, five rocks in the 12–13 pound range, and one or two that are larger. Most land in the oceans. Few are seen, and fewer are found. Out of maybe 500 large meteorites that reach the Earth each year, fewer than two dozen will ever be discovered.[14] The rates of random meteors varies by time of night and time of year. Meteors increase by 2–3 times after midnight, when we're facing the direction where Earth is headed. Fall meteors outnumber spring meteors by the same factor. You can expect 4–8 meteors per hour during a clear evening in March. But you'd enjoy early mornings in September even better, when the number doubles to 8–16 random meteors per hour.[15]

Meteor rates rise substantially during a shower, when the Earth passes through the dusty trails left behind by comets and asteroids. There are a dozen major dust trails that we revisit on each lap around the sun (plus 230 minor trails). Some showers produce mostly dim, fast meteors, while others feature meteors that are bright but slow. November's Leonid meteors strike the atmosphere at 44 miles/second (71 km/sec). The Draconid meteors in October arrive at a leisurely 14 miles/second (23 km/sec).[16] The difference in speed affects when the grains start glowing. Faster ones light up about 60 miles above the Earth's surface, but slower meteors don't become incandescent until they're 40 miles high, where the atmosphere is more dense. Ram pressure quickly slows them down to about the normal speed of a passenger jet. If anything is left, most meteors stop glowing and go dark somewhere between 20 and 5 miles high.[17] Their outer surface might get a little crusted, like toast, but meteors are typically cold when they hit the ground to become meteorites.[18]

Finding Meteorites in Glacier

To find meteorites in Glacier, you should first hike to a beautiful spot far from civilization. Search out a comfortable rock and rub your index finger across its upper surface. Then sit back and contemplate the dust on your finger tip while enjoying the view. Many of those dust grains recently arrived from space. Of course, you could wipe micro-meteorites from the dusty window sills around your house,[19] but why clean when you could be out hiking?

DUSTY STARS & SNOWBALLS

Meteorites and comets. They giveth and they taketh away.

Day in and day out, space dust and rocks deliver the basic ingredients needed for life on this little planet.[1,2,3] And then once every 100–400 million years, a cataclysmic meteorite strike wipes the planet nearly clean again.[4,5] The Earth quickly sprouts a range of new forms from the species that survive. Comets are capable of this same give and take,[6] but nothing much that's solid remains from snowball strikes, so they're often feared while meteorites are revered.[7]

Meteorites confounded early men of science and religion — fields where women were not allowed. Earth was the center of an orderly and manly universe, and surely the Big Man upstairs would not throw random stones at us. No, these strange rocks must have Earthly origins. Maybe they were ejected into high arcs from powerful volcanoes in some distant part of the world. Chemical analysis finally proved that these were not earthly stones. Meteorites were either rocks from space or messages from God.[8]

In Oregon, the 15-ton *Tomanowos*, or Willamette meteorite was discovered in 1902 and led a colorful history of theft, lawsuits, sale, and more lawsuits. Oregon's Grand Ronde tribe claims ownership, but it's possible that this meteorite didn't fall in Oregon. Evidence points to an original landing on a Canadian ice field that was sent bobbing west when an ice dam broke open on Glacial Lake Missoula.[9] These repeated floods inundated much of the northwest. The *Tomanowos* rested in Oregon for thousands of years, but this meteorite currently resides in New York City at the American Museum of Natural History.

Closer to home, a rare iron meteorite is venerated by traditional Native peoples east of the Continental Divide, in northern Montana and southern Alberta. This is just north of our current international border, where traditional Blackfoot territory pushed up against the southern boundary of the Cree tribes. Skirmishes pushed control of the region back and forth, and both tribes

hunted buffalo here. In this area, a 330-pound iron meteorite came to rest on a hill overlooking a small creek, in a place where members of both tribes visited and left offerings for the Great Spirit who sent this stone.

Some stories tell how, in October of 1809, a group of Cree were camped many miles to the east when a large fireball passed over them and fell towards the mountains. Scouts sent out the next morning discovered a reddish-brown meteor near the traditional hunting area.[10] Viewed from a certain angle, one side of this polished, 4.5 billion-year-old stone looks like the profile of a face. The Cree call it *pahpamiyhaw asiniy*, and the Blackfoot call it *Manitou*, the "Great Spirit Stone."[11]

In 1869, a Methodist minister stole the sacred Manitou Stone. He didn't appreciate the spiritual competition, so he hired a Red River cart and hauled the stone to his church 60 miles (97 km) away.[12] Native people took a dim view of this desecration.[13] That church building soon faded from the plains, and for many years the Manitou Stone bounced around between museums. It currently sits on display at the Royal Alberta

Museum in Edmonton. Representatives of the Canadian government and the First Nations are trying to find a compromise that will return the sacred stone to the area where it was discovered.[14]

Some of our other meteorites also have histories of bouncing around — between planets. Five million years ago, a massive meteorite or comet strike on Mars ejected rocky debris towards our planet. So far, we've discovered 124 of these Martian meteorite cast-offs on Earth.[15] We've also found 227 meteorites that were blasted to Earth from the moon.[16]

Earth flies into many more meteoroids than the heavily-cratered moon, but our atmosphere and weather erode and hide the evidence. Of the 60,000 meteorites that have been found on Earth, only seven have been discovered in Montana and all of these were in the southern portion of our state.[17] But Montana and Idaho share one of the largest of the Earth's 185 known impact craters. The cross-state Beaverhead Impact Structure is about 60 miles (95 km) in diameter, weather-worn and estimated at 600 million years old.[18] You can hike the Beaverhead crater, you just can't *see* it.

Meet Two Dusty Stars

If you'd like to meet a meteorite or see a comet, the best places to look are in dark, night skies and natural history museums. Unfortunately, all of the specimens from meteorites found in Montana currently belong to private collections and out-of-state institutions. I don't know of any meteorites larger than dust that still reside in Montana, but you can still meet and touch the Manitou Stone in Edmonton, Alberta.

You can also admire Glacier's stunning daytime meteorite that soars above Saint Mary Lake's west end. The Blackfeet name for Dusty Star Mountain is *Iszika-kakatosi*, which means "meteor" or "smoking star."[19] Smoking stars are visible in Glacier's dark skies on any clear night, and one or two dusty star comets are visible over the mountains each year.

*"**Comet Dust & Northern Lights**"* (above). An Orionid meteor streaks across the sky that's colored yellow with northern lights above Glacier National Park's Livingston mountain range.

*"**Comet Tail and Meteor Trail**"* (facing page). In the sky above Babb, a fiery meteor leaves a smoke trail just above 2014's Comet Lovejoy. This night was -21F/-29C, and there is blurry steam in the sky from the Saint Mary River, out of view in the foreground.

"Geminid Meteors and Northern Lights" *(above). Four faint Geminid meteors flash above a display of northern lights over Lake McDonald in mid-December.*

"Many Glacier Meteor" *(facing page). A random meteor falls in front of the Milky Way above Mount Gould, in the Many Glacier Valley.*

NEAR-EARTH ASTEROIDS

Meteoroids that are boulder-sized or larger are called asteroids. Lots of them fly past us every day without causing trouble. If they approach within 121 million miles (195 million km), then we call them near-Earth asteroids and pay more attention, but they're still farther from us than we are from the sun. We currently know of more than 12,000 near-Earth asteroids.[1] About half of these are thought to be "dead" comets that have run out of ice, leaving only rocky rubble.[2]

In the early morning hours of January 27, 2015, a near-Earth asteroid (2004 BL86) buzzed us within 745,000 miles (1.2 million km) of Earth, about three times the distance between us and the moon. This asteroid is only about 1,100 feet (325 m) wide, but it isn't lonely in space. On that morning it revealed that it is accompanied by a small moon that's 230 feet (70 m) wide.[3] About 16% of all near-Earth asteroids have one or two companions,[4] and many asteroids are clumps of rubble. The next pass of a *known* near-Earth asteroid will occur in 2027, but asteroid 2004 BL86 won't visit us again for another two centuries.[5]

Finding Your Asteroid

If you know where and when to look, you can watch asteroids passing through the dark night skies above Glacier National Park. Asteroids move faster than background stars and slower than artificial satellites, but most are too dim to see with naked eyes. You can use binoculars, but a telescope is your best bet.

"Shining Asteroid" (above). A near-Earth asteroid (2004 BL86) swings past the Beehive star cluster in the early morning of January 27, 2015. The asteroid shows up as dashes in this interval photograph.

Wandering Planets & Son of Morning Star

One group of stars stood above the rest to Old World sky watchers. These stars traveled the sky on a much different path, so the ancient Greeks called these *planetes asteres*,[1] or "wandering stars." They named the *planetes* after Roman gods and revered them alongside the sun and moon. Two centuries later they realized that the morning and evening stars were the same thing, but the Greeks never knew that the wandering stars they deified were actually five planets.

The two brightest planets, Venus and Jupiter, play major roles in the most important Blackfoot story of all. Morning Star (Venus) is the son of Sun and Moon. Morning Star's son is Star Child (Jupiter), from the union with his Blackfoot wife, *So-at-sa-ki,*

or "Feather Woman." Star Child's adult name changed to *Poia*, or "Scar Face."[2,3,4]

Feather Woman was a virtuous young woman who declined proposals from many young men. Sleeping under the stars, she awoke and fell in love with Morning Star, saying aloud that she would take the handsome Star as her husband. A few months later, she found herself with child and scorned by her tribe. Morning Star appeared in human form, saying that he had accepted her marriage offer. They moved into the Sky World to raise their son.

Feather Woman was happy with her new husband and son, but she missed her parents and tribe. Digging up the sacred root that Moon told her to

leave alone, she saw through this hole to her old camp on the ground below. For this misbehavior she and Star Child (*Poia*) were banished back to Earth. Even though Star Child had been born in the sky, he was left poor and alone on Earth after his Blackfoot family died. As a young man, *Poia* was mistreated and spurned by everyone, including the young maiden that he loved. She would not marry him unless he removed the scar (symbolic of the imperfect human condition).[5] For this, an old medicine woman said he must travel back to the Sun. It was a long and difficult journey.

Sun was not pleased to see *Poia*, but Moon allowed him to stay and Morning Star promised to take care of him. He proved to be a brave hunter, and Sun decided to remove his scar and make *Poia* a messenger to the Blackfoot. He learned the sacred ceremonies to share with his people. *Poia* followed the Wolf's Trail back to his tribe and married the beautiful maiden. After teaching the Sun Dance to the Blackfoot, *Poia* and his wife moved into the sky. Sun was pleased and made *Poia* into a bright star — just like his father.

Venus and Jupiter Wanderings

The orbits of father and son differ quite a bit. Venus circles the sun in 225 Earth days, while Jupiter orbits at a much slower pace of 4,332 days. They meet in the sky about every 13 months (see *Sky Events*), and these conjunctions repeat in 24-year cycles.[6] Venus is eight times brighter than Jupiter, and both are visible in daytime if you know when to look. Venus orbits between us and the sun, so they never appear very far apart in our sky. When trailing the sun, Venus grows impressive right after sunset. When it's ahead of the sun, Venus stands apart until dawn.[7]

Modern Jupiter is sometimes called the king of planets, a mini solar system and a would-be star. The other seven planets combined would amount to less than two-thirds of Jupiter's mass. It holds a fleet of 67 moons, including asteroids captured by its massive gravity. Jupiter's gravity generates more internal heat that it receives from the sun, but this giant gas still only has 1/80th of the mass needed to fuse hydrogen like a star.[8,9,10]

"Jupiter Over Cut Bank." *Jupiter glows silently over the Cut Bank Valley just before a January dawn, while the light dome over Flathead Valley (45 air miles to the west) reflects from a bank of low clouds. Sky glow aurora is also visible if you look closely.*

"Jupiter Rising." *While a pickup drives along the North Fork Road at midnight, Jupiter slowly rises in a notch between Glacier View Mountain (left) and Huckleberry Mountain (right). Thirty minutes of star trails form the background for a single image of Jupiter, which is reflected in the North Fork River.*

Eclipsed Realities

The original definition of "eclipse" means to quit or disappear. Now we use the term when one space body disappears or passes behind another from our view. The moon blocks our view of the sun during a solar eclipse, and the Earth shades the moon during a lunar eclipse. But it's good to keep the original definition in mind when watching eclipses from Glacier National Park, where the sun and moon often disappear behind clouds.

A 1782 solar eclipse and an 1889 lunar eclipse were recorded on the same Blackfoot winter count (Bull Plume).[1,2] A lunar eclipse graced Glacier National Park in May of 1910, when the park was just 13 days old.

My first eclipse in Glacier came a few years later, in May of 2000, when the crescent moon passed in front of a crescent Venus (facing page). I hauled my family up North Fork that morning, and the orbs emerged from clouds just in time. In 2010, I tried photographing the December 20 lunar eclipse over Lake McDonald. Four hours into my time-lapse, clouds moved in just as the eclipse was finally starting. I turned my cameras off and watched. My next opportunity arrived in May 2013, and the skies were miraculously clear. But I had trouble standing in the 40 mph (64 km/hr) wind. So did my tripod. Dawn arrived a few minutes too early, and that's when I realized that I'd bumped a camera dial with the cast on my thumb.

During a partial solar eclipse in October 2014 I went so far as to make a test image the day before ("Kiss the Sun," page 4). But a front moved in overnight and a downpour smothered the northern Rockies. Rain chased me 50 miles onto the plains, where I captured half of the eclipse behind an old grain silo. Then the rain caught up again. Those are the days that I have to remind myself of the old eclipse stories.

On the 29th of July, 1878, a spectacular solar eclipse swept down the Rocky Mountains, across western Montana and onward to Wyoming and Colorado. A dry, two-page report was issued out of Helena,[3] but the better story originated from Rawlins, Wyoming. Professional astronomers picked this town as *the* prime location, and they claimed the best spots to set up their telescopes out of the wind. A 31-year-old inventor with a familiar name, Thomas Edison, was left to poke his telescope through the roof opening in a small chicken coop. Using his newest invention, a super-sensitive thermometer called a tasimeter, he set out to measure the temperature of the mysterious flares that are only visible during less than two minutes of totality.

Edison frantically began dialing in his equipment as the sky turned dark. At this critical moment, chickens began fluttering in through the same opening. Fooled by a false dusk, the chickens were coming home to roost. Edison still managed to record a temperature that proved the corona was part of the sun, not lunar atmosphere. It was a year later that he patented his incandescent light bulb. A few years after that, papers turned up from an earlier eclipse in 1842. A professor in Italy had previously measured the coronal temperature, eclipsing Edison by 36 years.[4]

My favorite eclipse story is told by Timothy Ferris, in *Coming of Age in the Milky Way*.[5] Venus was set to cross the sun's face in 1761, and

"Lunar Eclipse." *A partial lunar eclipse on December 11, 2011, shades the full moon as it fades into dawn between Yellow Mountain East and Chief Mountain.*

many governments sent their top astronomers to distant countries to time this event. By combining all of the timings they could finally triangulate the distance to the sun. Guillaume le Gentil sailed from France a year early to time the transit from India. But they were blown off course, and he was left floating on a rocking ship on the critical date. He proceeded to India anyway, determined to time the next transit of Venus eight years later, in 1769.

Gentil built a fine observatory in India and enjoyed sunny blue skies until June 4th, the morning of the second transit. One cloud crossed the sun until just after the transit was over, then the skies cleared.

Gentil felt crushed, and that's when he contracted dysentery. Nine bedridden months later, he boarded a ship that lost a mast in a hurricane and was later blown off course in the Azores. He disembarked in Spain, crossed the Pyrenees on foot, and finally arrived back in France 11 years and 6 months after leaving. Gentil had accomplished nothing but he was finally home, where he discovered that his family had long since declared him dead and divvied up all of his possessions. That's when Gentil quit astronomy.

Facing Reality

Only 10 total solar eclipses have cast shadows across the mainland U.S. in the last 100 years, and only two of those touched Montana.[6] The 1945 "Victory Eclipse" crossed over Butte at 5 a.m.[7], and the 1979 eclipse arrived on a dreary, cloudy day.[8] Let's hope for more reasonable weather for three partial solar eclipses that will be visible from Glacier in 2017 (85% eclipsed), 2023 (68% eclipsed) and 2024 (29% eclipsed)[9,10,11] During 2015–2024, there will also be at least one lunar eclipse visible from Glacier every year except 2023. See the *Sky Events* section for dates and times.

Solar and lunar eclipses are events that need to be witnessed, not just read about in a book. On any given day, the chance for clouds is moderate in a mountainous area like Glacier National Park. But considering just how rare and spectacular eclipses are in person, the reward is worth the risk.

"Venus Moon." *A crescent Venus passes behind a crescent Moon in the morning sky. This type of eclipse is known as an "occultation." This is an interval photograph, with frames made one minute apart, that I actually made from a hillside in the North Fork Valley. I had optimistically, and mistakenly, thought I would be able to include Glacier's Livingston Range in the photograph. It was a lovely idea, however.*

URSA MAJOR NOCTURNE

You almost have to tell a bear story when you're ruminating on Glacier National Park.

My wife and I never seem to have enough time for our small circle of friends, an earthy group of teacher and ranger types. At a rare summer get-together, Tracy was complaining (in a loving way) about some of the hazards of being a photographer's assistant. I enjoy the challenges of night photography more than she does, but Tracy's a good sport about it. So I listened silently while she told her version of what transpired a few nights earlier, on Glacier's east side.

We started work at about midnight with a little one-mile, full-moon hike through excellent bear habitat so I could try a light painting project that I'd been thinking about all winter. We took turns calling out, *"Hey Bear! Hey Moosey-moose!"* Volume matters far more than content. I prefer silence, but it's not a good idea to surprise a big, wild animal — especially in the dark.[1,2,3]

After the light painting we moved on to photograph the moonset over a lake. How romantic of me, I thought. After the moon dropped below the horizon, the sky was dark enough to try for star trail photos on yet another lake. By then it was 3:30 a.m. and Tracy was half asleep. But it was still pretty dark, so I wanted to squeeze in one more light painting at a spot where the road crosses a roaring creek.

Tracy stood beside the bridge and slightly below the road, and I was upstream and uphill, painting light onto my subject with a big flashlight. Her job was to trip the camera shutter open, watch a stopwatch for 60 seconds, and then close the shutter. While she sleepily watched the seconds count down, my sudden commotion caught her attention.

"Hey Bear!" I yelled and clambered downhill towards her, with my bear spray drawn. That woke her up.

Just beyond Tracy, an adult grizzly was strolling silently along the road. I angled to get between the bear and Tracy, making sure he wouldn't turn up the

trail and encounter my favorite assistant. Tracy drew her bear spray and jumped to my side.

"Hey Bear!" we yelled in duet.

In spite of all our yelling, the bear paid no attention to us whatsoever. He just wanted to cross the creek without getting wet. After our visitor reached the far side of the bridge and disappeared back into the dark, I turned back to the photo at hand.

"Did you close the shutter?" I asked.

Maybe it was the lack of sleep, but when Tracy saw the grizzly bear she forgot all about my photograph. I closed the shutter while Tracy stared intently down the dark road. *"I don't suppose you still want to hike down the trail to the waterfall,"* I tried. She declined. Instead, she declared that we were taking the rest of the night off. She was shaking, and it really didn't feel all that cold out.

While Tracy recounted her bear encounter with our old friends, I was watching out of the corner of my eye for any sort of reaction from Gary, the ranger who got called in for many bear maulings in the park. He just shook his head.

"Be careful," he told me, *"I don't wanna have to patch you up."*

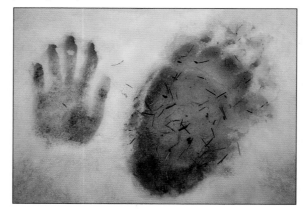

See Bears in the Dark

Just kidding. Please leave our bears in peace. Bears are most active at dawn and dusk, though they do have individual preferences just like us. Bears like to use park trails for energy-efficient travel. If you're a night owl like me, don't set up shop near a trail or along a lake shore. Make noise from time to time, especially during windy or moonless nights. Don't wear smelly perfumes, shampoos or deodorants, because a bear follows its nose to unfamiliar scents.[4,5]

Always, always, always carry pepper spray, and keep it in easy reach (not buried in your pack). Handguns are legal to carry in the park (illegal to fire), but pepper spray has repeatedly proven to be the better deterrent in surprise encounters.[6,7,8] The canisters don't spray well in freezing temperatures,[9] but the big bears only venture out occasionally in the winter. Bear spray can save your hide, but its main purpose is to save the bear's life if you mess up. Bears live in the park, and we're just visitors.

If you're determined to see bears at night, I know of two that I can point out in Glacier. Fortunately, it's still pretty easy to see a Great Bear and a Little Bear in the park's dark night skies.

If you can find the Big Dipper, that is an asterism that belongs to a Ursa Major, the Great Bear constellation. The dipper handle is the bear's extra-long tail (this anatomical indiscretion comes courtesy of ancient astronomers, not biologists). On the opposite end, the dipper's front two stars guide us towards a polar bear of sorts.

Drawing a line from these two stars leads you to Polaris, the north polar star. Polaris is the last star in the Little Dipper's handle, and also the last star in the Little Bear constellation, Ursa Minor. Except for Polaris, the Little Bear's seven stars are faint and hard to see. You'll need a good, dark sky, like the one over Glacier Park. These days, light pollution keeps both of these bears from showing up at night over our larger towns and cities.

"Grizzly Trail" (left). A grizzly sow and her yearling stroll down Many Glacier Road on a snowy morning before dawn.

"Hand and Foot" (facing page). My handprint in the snow compared to the size of an imprint left by a black bear's left rear foot.

"Who Nose" (below). A male black bear (right member of the pair) carefully approaches a female before dawn in the Lee Creek drainage on the east side of Glacier. During mating season the young couple will travel together for several days before parting ways.

CREATURES OF THE NIGHT

The U.S. population is currently growing at 1.5% annually, but the average rate of light growth is 6% per year. This amounts to a doubling of light pollution every 10 years, 11 months.[1] A worldwide average of 3% light growth means doubling light pollution every 23 years.[2] Too much artificial light at night is no longer just an issue for astronomers and dreamers, like me. These nights, light pollution negatively affects nearly every form of life on our little planet.[3, 4]

Light is a very good thing. The problem is that light at night is *unnatural*. The vast majority of earthly animal and plant life forms are hormonally programmed for one long, uninterrupted period of darkness during each 24-hour cycle.[5,6] Light pollution causes behavioral and biological reactions that fly in the face of three billion years of *natural* light/dark cycles. This messes up behavioral cues in insects, frogs, birds, mammals, etc. And for us, too much light after sunset triggers a series of hormonal effects that, unlike the light itself, can be toxic or fatal.[7,8,9]

Why do moths fly into your porch lights over and over? Because just like us, moths evolved with natural darkness that didn't include bright artificial lights. Most moth species use the moon as a distant, unreachable navigation point.[10] Flying at the moon means flying in a straight line. This is an energy-efficient strategy when males are sniffing out females, and when females are searching for specific plant species for egg-laying. But it's far less effective when you actually thump your brain on the brightest light in the new night sky. Moths attracted to lights tend to land nearby and remain there all night instead of doing what moths normally do, like pollinate flowers and feed bats.

Moth numbers have fallen by more than 66% in some countries during the last 40 years.[11] Changes in moth species compositions can cause a decline in night-flowering plant species, changing the surrounding plant community.[12] Light trespass also rudely interferes with lightning bug mating signals (flashes).[13] In experiments, female frogs ignored high-quality male calls from dimly-lit areas, moving instead towards low-quality male calls from dark areas.[14] Electric lights can also disorient those hard-working dung beetles who use the moon and Milky Way to navigate at night[15] — and who would want to take over *that* job?

American robins in light-polluted areas begin singing earlier in the morning, while it's still night.[16] Buildings glowing at night can confuse and blind migrating and local birds. For birds flying at night without electric lights, dark areas are trees and mountains, and the open sky is brighter. Buildings with lit-up interiors reverse the visual cues.

Crepuscular and nocturnal animals are susceptible to "deer in the headlights" blindness. Headlights instantly saturate their rod cells and leave them effectively blind. They can't see where to run to evade your car, and after you pass by they can't spot potential predators in the dark until their night vision slowly returns 20–40 minutes later.

Just like insects and mammals, plants are also programmed for uninterrupted darkness. Most plants photosynthesize in daylight, but it's darkness that actually controls shoot growth, flowering and dormancy. The ratio of daylight to darkness, or photoperiodism, also affects root development, leaf shape and pigment formation. Most plants have a light-sensitive pigment called cytochrome that can be disrupted by even a short flash of light.[17]

Artificial light in the red to infrared wavelengths can also trick trees into keeping their leaves into winter, when the weight of falling snow can break off their branches.[18] And if trees delay the withdrawal of sap into underground roots, freezing air temperatures can expand and crack their branches and trunks. As it is, it gets so cold in still-dark Glacier that I often hear tree limbs cracking and popping on especially frigid, below-zero nights.

In the U.S. alone, we waste an estimated $10 billion each year on poorly-aimed lights. Unshielded lights dump 17 billion kilowatt-hours into the sky and create those ugly, orange clouds over our towns and cities, wasting $2 billion annually.[19] Literature reviews point out that crime levels are statistically unrelated to the number of lumens poured into parking lots and street lamps,[20] and most burgularies occur during daylight.[21] Proper lighting doesn't mean pouring on more light, it means using light more effectively.

Of course, many things are more precious than money. Light pollution silently degrades our priceless quality of life. On top of sleep disorders, artificial light is now implicated in obesity, diabetes, cardiovascular ailments and cancer. In 2009 the American Medical Association confirmed that artificial light after sunset can suppress melatonin production. A drop in melatonin translates into depressed immune systems and increased cancer rates, especially breast cancers. Research shows an "unequivocal positive association" between breast cancer and bedroom light levels.[22]

Research by the National Institutes of Health documented disruptions in melatonin production among night shift workers, like nurses, and determined that night shifts are "probably carcinogenic to humans."[23] In laboratory mice, even small amounts of light at night accelerated aging and stimulated cancer.[24]

Nurturing Natural Darkness

Most people are smarter than moths and mice. We don't have to keep damaging our brains with night lights. Awareness of the issue is the first step back towards the place where the human race spent its formative years — in Earth's natural shadow at night. Many of the steps are easy and free, and some will even save money. I've included *Lighting Basics* and *Resources* sections in the back of this book to help get you started.

"Montana Six-plumed Moth." *A Montana six-plumed moth (Alucita montana) rests on a rusty pipe in West Glacier. Instead of scaled wings, this moth flies on overlapping plumes that resemble feathers. Its quarter-inch wingspan is the width of Lincoln on a U.S. copper penny. Glacier is 100+ years old but its native moth species have not been identified.*

MOUNTAIN MOONSETS

The moon as seen from a mountain setting
is unlike the moon in any other foreground,
and mountains in moonlight are marvelously beautiful.

Morton Elrod ~ Glacier National Park, 1924[1]

"Apgar Moonset." A nearly-full moon sets behind Apgar Village in an interval photograph over Lake McDonald.

Morton Elrod certainly knew a thing or two about Glacier National Park, long before the park officially existed. As head of the science department at the University of Montana, Elrod made frequent trips to the area, where he studied plants, animals, insects and anything else that captured his curiousity. He established UM's biological station on Flathead Lake in 1899, helped launch the National Bison Range and pushed Congress to create Montana's mountain park[2] in 1910. The National Park Service hired Elrod in 1922 as Glacier's first official naturalist, and he built Glacier's first museum and herbarium. Elrod earned a salary of $100 per month for his seasonal service. He also sold postcards to tourists, supplementing the income from his park and university employment to feed his young family.[3]

Elrod clipped and saved a 1911 newspaper story of a large meteor that passed over western Montana, heading north towards the new park.[4] He wrote volumes about the park's mountain passes, glaciers, lakes, flowers and animals.[5] Elrod's most popular work by far was a little 5-inch book simply called, *Elrod's Guide & Book of Information*. First published in 1924, this was Glacier's first guidebook and was soon known as the must-read "bible" for visitors to the new park.[6]

Dr. George Ruhle succeeded Elrod in 1929 to become Glacier's first permanent, year-round naturalist. This former professor with a PhD in nuclear physics was soon pushing a bicycle wheel and cyclometer over the 1,000 miles (1,610 km) or so of Glacier's trails to produce his spiral-bound *Guide to Glacier* in 1949, which was the official update to *Elrod's Guide* and the new must-read for park visitors.[7] Ruhle's popular guide was republished three times and updated once again in 1972 as *The Roads and Trails of Waterton-Glacier National Parks*.

I cherish my yellowed, first-edition copy of *Elrod's Guide*. Sometimes when I'm stuck at home on cloudy nights, I like to thumb through and imagine Glacier's landscapes through Elrod's eyes — including the moonrises that left an emotional impression on such a man of science.

Thumb Through History

Blackfoot Lodge Tales was well worth its $1.00 price when George Bird Grinnell first published it in 1913.[8] Some of my favorite books are listed in the *Resources* section. The National Park Service at Glacier maintains a museum collection, archives and the George C. Ruhle Library that are open to the public. Appointments are recommended.

"Moonset Over Saint Mary River." *The glowing full moon kisses Chief Mountain and reflects off murmuring waves and riffles in the Saint Mary River. The traditional Blackfoot name for this river is* Ahkai'nuskwona Iye'tuktai, *or "Many Chiefs Gathered River." This name refers back to a long-ago gathering and council of the chiefs from the Blackfoot tribes, the Gros Ventres, several west-side tribes, and others.*[9]

"Sore Eyes Moon." *A 6% crescent moon slips below the clouds and into a saddle on the north side of Mount Henkel. The peak was named for a pioneer in the Saint Mary Lake area, Joseph Henkel. The Blackfeet called him* Ikaipini, *or "Red Sore Eyes."*[10]

"Wild Goose Moon and Stars." *A setting moon outlines Wild Goose Island and reveals the night stars above Saint Mary Lake. A traditional Blackfeet story says that the Wind Maker lives underwater at the head of this lake. He makes the wind blow by rolling massive waves towards the east.[8] If you have ever spent any time at Saint Mary Lake, you know that the area is almost always windy.*

"Swiftcurrent Lookout." *A full moon at dawn slips silently behind the fire lookout on Swiftcurrent Peak. To reach the precise camera location where this would line up, I had to head up the trail in the dark hours before dawn. I arrived to discover that the tree canopy was too thick, and I had to move downslope to find an opening, which is why there is slightly less than half of the moon showing above the mountaintop.*

"Moonset Blues." *Moonlight still paints the sky blue after setting over Two Medicine Lake just past midnight. This is a light painting photograph, where I used a flashlight to illuminate the underwater rocks during a long exposure.*

SOLAR RAYS & MOON BEAMS

Hello, good morning! (English).

Oki, i'taamikskanaotonni! (Blackfoot).[1]

Way xast lkʷkʷʔast! (Salish).[2]

Some days the sun greets us playfully with shafts of light. Not only does the sun make impressive beams while it's still below the horizon, but sometimes the sun and moon also shine spotlights through broken clouds when they're a little ways above the horizon.

On mostly clear days, when the sun is barely below the horizon, sunlight that's broken into beams and shadows by mountains or clouds (on your horizon or beyond) are called crepuscular rays. When these rays reach from the opposite horizon, we call them anticrepuscular rays.

Crepuscular rays appear to converge at the source, but they're really parallel. We're fooled by the same perspective that appears to make both sides of a long road come together. Crepuscular rises from *"crepusculum,"* the Latin word for twilight.

On cloudy days, when the sun or moon is above the horizon, they might send beams around the edges and through the holes in clouds. We call these solar rays, sun beams or moon beams. Like crepuscular rays, they appear to converge at the source, but they're actually parallel to each other.[3]

"Moon Clouds." Sunlight reflecting off the moon shines beams around the edges of a broken cloud near Chief Mountain, just before sunrise.

"Crepuscular Rays" (top) peek over the Livingston Range at 5 a.m, and 35 minutes later, *"Solar Rays"* (bottom) poke through the clouds at 6 a.m.

66

PAINTING ON CLOUDS

If you're going to watch night skies in Glacier, you'd better learn to like clouds. The sun will do its part to help you. Dawn and dusk on partly-cloudy days are the best times for cloud colors. Relative to sunrise and sunset, clouds turn colorful in the order of their altitude — high to low.[1]

High-level, wispy clouds (cirrus, cirrocumulus, cirrostratus) are the first to light up in the pre-dawn, and the last to fade at dusk. Made of ice crystals, they can turn orange or red 10–20 minutes before sunrise or after sunset. The atmosphere needs to be exceptionally clear for cirro-form clouds to grow very colorful.

Mid-level clouds (altocumulus, altostratus, nimbostratus) are usually flat-bottomed cotton balls with distinct edges. They can blush 5–10 minutes before sunrise or after sunset. The air needs to have enough air-borne dust to scatter the light waves, but not so much dust to form haze.

Low-level clouds (cumulus, stratus, strato-cumulus, cumulonimbus) are made of water droplets. They're the most likely to cause a case of jaw drop because low clouds are the closest to you. Haze will have little effect on their brightest colors, right at sunrise and sunset. As usual, the most intense events last the shortest time.

*"**Divide Moon at Dawn.**" A last-quarter moon watches low-level stratocumulus clouds turn orange at dawn over Divide Mountain, near Saint Mary. Divide Mountain is a sacred site to the Blackfoot. This peak briefly held the name "White Calf Mountain" during 1896–97, but Divide is the older name.[2]*

RETURNING TO THE SUN

There are no foothills east of *Miistakis*, the "Backbone of the World," just rolling plains lapping at the feet of mountains. The morning sun greets the tallest of these mountains in splashes of red before climbing down the lower peaks to warm the shadowed plains below. Among these sentinels stands one that some Blackfoot regard as their most beautiful peak (after Chief Mountain). They once knew it as *Nitai' Ispi Istuki*, or "Lone High Mountain."[3] But the original name was changed during a bout of poetic license by

the man the Blackfoot entrusted to record their original names.[4] His story illustrates our complex history of place names.

Long before Glacier National Park existed, local people already had names for many of these mountains, names that were maintained in oral histories but not necessarily written down.[5,6] When Europeans flooded across these plains and mountains, innudating local cultures, the turbulence was especially hard on the Blackfoot.

In July 1877, a self-described "foolish tenderfoot" named James Willard Schultz rode this wave into these mountains. Astride a buffalo horse, he carried a bedroll, a .44 caliber Henry rifle, and a leather pouch filled with tobacco.[7] Not quite 18 years old, Schultz was a young white man from New York state who'd ridden the steamers 2,600 miles from St. Louis to Fort Benton, as far up the Missouri River as paddle boats could go. He found employment as a trader — buffalo (bison) hides mostly. He and Joe Kitt purchased locally

"Going to the Sun." *While Mount Reynolds waits in twilight, Going-to-the-Sun Mountain reaches for the first rays of sunlight on a winter morning. Blackfoot once knew this mountain as,* Nitai' Ispi Istuki, *or "Lone High Mountain."* [1,2]

tanned hides for $3 each, selling them in St. Louis for $7 each.[8] In 1879, Schultz married *Natahki*, a young Blackfeet woman. They lived among her tribe during 1880–82 before building a little ranch to raise cattle. Schultz learned the local language, joined the Blackfeet in raids against their enemies, and came to see the country through native eyes. The Pikuni chief, Running Crane, gave Schultz a Blackfeet name, *Apikuni*, or "White-far-off-Robe."[9]

During the mid-1880s, Schultz started guiding visitors into the wild *Miistakis* that we now call Glacier National Park. He became friends with a young anthropologist who was the editor of *Field & Stream* magazine. George Bird Grinnell hired Schultz to write articles about the Blackfeet and these mountains.[10] Schultz became an accomplished guide and prolific writer. He joined Grinnell's efforts to promote the idea of a nation's park along the rocky *Miistakis*. Some critics have accused Schultz of romanticizing Indian life, and he was often guilty of straying from any facts or dates that he found ill-fitting.[11] But his first-person stories would become well-loved around the world, including in Blackfeet country, in spite of his occasional transgressions.[12]

While Grinnell set to mapping these mountains, Schultz led the effort to document the original names for these peaks, lakes and waterfalls. Grinnell succeeded in 1910, when Congress officially designated part of the area as Glacier National Park. The new land managers started printing maps that gave new names for many of the park's features, much to the disgust of the locals. One of them, Tail-Feathers-Coming-Over-the-Hill, said that the whites were trying to erase ancient Blackfeet history by renaming landmarks with "foolish names of no meaning whatsoever."[13]

Schultz camped regularly with Blackfeet elders on the shores of Two Medicine Lake, and in 1925 this "council of old men"[14] gathered around the fire inside Curly Bear's sacred Beaver Medicine Lodge to formulate a plan. They would ask Kootenai and other west side tribes to document the original names for 153 Glacier National Park features west of the divide, and Schultz would help the Blackfeet document their names east of the divide. They would also give new Indian names to the features that had no historic name.[15] Led by Schultz, the

group agreed upon 40 traditional names for 161 east side features in Glacier park.[16] One of these was the ancient Indian path over what we now call Logan Pass, known from the earliest times as *Misum Oksokwi*, or "Old Road."[17]

The council was left with more than 100 features that either had no name, or the name couldn't be agreed upon. They set about naming these places mostly for famous chiefs from the old buffalo days, but Schultz also gave some places fanciful new titles. One of these was the old "Lone High Mountain." Schultz made up a colorful legend to go along with his new name for the place that he called *Natosi-aitapo*, "Sun Going-to Mountain."[18,19]

Schultz faced opposition from a few of the newcomers. During the 1890s, Dr. Lyman Sperry had named many west side features for colleges and white professors. Sperry allowed that some of the east side features might be renamed, so long

as the old Indian names were easy to pronounce, and his new west side names were left intact.[20] (Sperry's name would become attached to a west side glacier in 1929.) In 1926, Schultz published the native place names in *Signposts of Adventure: Glacier National Park as the Indians Know It*. In 1938 Glacier's first permanent naturalist, Dr. George C. Ruhle, returned 48 of the original names to Glacier's landmarks, almost entirely on the park's east side.[21,22] The old "Lone High Mountain" and, eventually, a road climbing over the wild *Miistakis* would come to be known as Going-to-the-Sun.

After his death in 1947, Schultz's remains were returned to his beloved plains along the *Miistakis*, where he was laid to rest alongside *Natahki*.[23,24] Today a mountain, creek, waterfall and major geologic formation all bear his Blackfoot name, *Apikuni*. At the head of Apikuni Creek lie the tranquil waters of Natahki Lake.[25]

"Mount Stimson Sunrise." At dawn a high-elevation gale blows snow from the peak of Mount Stimson. The peak was named for Henry Stimson, who helped George Bird Grinnell survey the area. The Kootenai called it "Flint Lodge," and the Blackfeet referred to it as the aerie of Thunder Eagle.[26]

"Red Lining" (top). Dawn lines clouds red over the Livingston mountain range.
"Sunrise" (above). An orange cloud hovers over Mount Gould at sunrise.
"Icy Pyramid" (right). Mount Saint Nicholas reaches for the morning sunshine.

"Heaven on Earth." *Sunbeams push through clouds above Heavens Peak in Glacier's Livingston Range, and spotlight the North Fork Valley. This image was made about 40 minutes after the "Red Lining" photograph on the facing page. Both images were made after I had spent all night standing on top of Glacier View Mountain, waiting for the clouds to part so I could photograph the Milky Way (see "Tree Snag," page 73).*

CAUTION LIGHTS & PROGRESS

Glacier National Park's largest natural resource, its naturally dark night sky, is slipping away. But growing numbers of park enthusiasts are taking notice, and we're starting to see steps taken to bring back the night.

The National Park Service modeled the night sky darkness across the U.S. from data collected in 1990.[1] Back then, the dark skies above Glacier National Park were rated as "pristine" (Schaff class 7).[2] A more recent worldwide mapping project that used data collected in 2006. It bumped Glacier's night sky down a notch but found it still within 94% of natural darkness.[3]

Both of these maps showed extensive light pollution on three sides of Glacier: the growing population centers of southern Alberta (Cardston, Lethbridge, Calgary), Montana's Flathead Valley (Kalispell, Whitefish, Columbia Falls), and to a lesser degree the towns and communities along the east front (Cut Bank, Browning, Babb). The artificial clouds of light pollution above our towns have crept into Glacier's horizons. As far as I know, there is no longer any backcountry wilderness location in Glacier National Park that is not affected by light pollution. The cone cells in our eyes are less sensitive than cameras to this yellowish-orange glow, but the trend is clear.

When you stand on the Apgar Beach and look to the north on a clear night, you can see yellow light from Canadian towns glowing above the crags of Glacier's Garden Wall. If you move to Lake McDonald's north shore and look south, the Flathead Valley's orange cloud colors your horizon. This same cloud is visible when you stop along Highway 89 and look west into the Cut Bank Valley. The orange even shows up in night photographs made from the Chief Mountain overlook, 55 air miles from Whitefish. Chief Mountain and its local clouds often reflect orange from the sodium vapor "security" lights around Babb. (See illustrations 1–4 on following pages.)

Fortunately, concerned citizens and scientists are working along several fronts to dial down the artificial light that trespasses into Glacier's night skies. Glacier National Park's management recently gave the green light to apply for International Dark Sky Park status, and to develop lighting guidelines that are a part of this process. These goals were written into management objectives, but no funding was provided. So the non-profit Glacier National Park Conservancy grabbed the reigns,[4] and I expect Glacier to reap the benefits of their work within a few years. Between 2007 and 2014, only 20 locations qualified for International Dark Sky Park status. In the U.S., these include four regional and six state parks, three national parks, two national monuments and one national historical park. If Glacier qualifies for this honor, it will join the likes of Death Valley and Big Bend National Parks, Hovenweep and Natural Bridges National Monuments, and Chaco Culture National Historical Park.[5]

These fledgling efforts probably wouldn't survive without nurturing support from the non-profit Dark Sky Association, founded in 1988. Starting in 1999, a NPS-based Night Sky Team began quantifying the darkness levels over 64 national parks, and they started up the NPS Night Sky Program interpretive events. Now more than a dozen U.S. national parks feature these night sky programs.[6] Volunteers in Glacier offer night sky viewing opportunities from Saint Mary and Apgar, solar-viewing from Apgar, and a star party at Logan Pass. Waterton Lakes also offers star parties at Cameron Lake.

Things here are looking up in our night skies above the Glacier/Waterton Backbone of the World — literally.

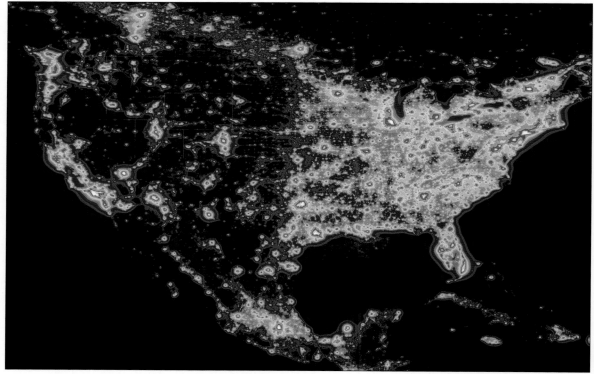

"2006 U.S. Night Sky Atlas." *Data used to produce this 2006 atlas are from the Operational Linescan System flown on Defense Meteorological Satellite Program satellites (credit: David Lorenz).*

(Above, left to right) Examples of light pollution in Glacier National Park:

"Tree Snag." A summer Milky Way fades into the dome of light from Columbia Falls and Kalispell.

"Cloudy Milky Way." Orange clouds from sodium vapor "safety" lights in nearby Babb cover up parts of the Milky Way above Chief Mountain.

"Lake McDonald at Midnight." Lake McDonald Lodge sits quietly at midnight, while the Flathead Valley's yellow light dome covers Glacier's southwestern corner.

"Lake McDonald Lodge." Unshielded fixtures at Lake McDonald Lodge currently allow light to escape into the treetops and beyond. This is the light that creates sky glow and hides stars. Hopefully, this kind of lighting will soon be corrected in Glacier National Park.

Bortle Scale Illustrations

In 2006, John Bortle published a 1–9 scale for amateur astronomers to use when estimating night sky darkness.[1] I'm a visually-oriented person, so in the following four illustrations, I used the Bortle scale built into the desktop planetarium Stellarium to give some idea of what Glacier National Park's night skies might look like if light pollution continues to grow inside and outside of the park. These illustrations may be imprecise, but they do illustrate what we stand to lose. They also illustrate how many stars you've lost from view if you live in a town (5) or city (9).

Bortle scale:
(1) excellent dark-sky site, (2) typical truly dark site, (3) rural sky, (4) rural/suburban transition, (5) suburban sky, (6) bright suburban sky, (7) suburban/urban transition, (8) city sky, (9) inner-city sky.[2]

Bortle 1 (current)   Bortle 3   Bortle 5   Bortle 7   Bortle 9

Illustration 1. *The night sky over Lake McDonald has been replaced with the sky chart from Stellarium. From left to right, our current night sky darkness is just above a Bortle scale 1 (far left). This represents an excellent dark sky location. A Bortle 3 location has lost some of the fainter stars, and this would represent a rural sky. Bortle 5 has lost most of the fainter stars, representing a suburban or small-town sky. In a Bortle 7 night sky, the Milky Way is lost, as are most of the stars. And in a Bortle 9 night sky (far right), only a handfull of the brightest stars are visible through the artificial glow.*

If the amount of artificial light continues to increase from the Calgary complex to the north, the night sky view over Lake McDonald will get pushed up the Bortle scale of light pollution, from the left side of this illustration towards the right side.

Photograph of Milky Way with blue-green sky glow at Logan Pass.

Stellarium illustration of same scene without sky glow (Bortle 1).

Bortle 5

Bortle 9

Illustration 2. *The night sky over Logan Pass has been replaced with a sky chart from Stellarium. Removing the natural sky glow illustrates our current Bortle scale 1 night sky (top right). Countless stars show on a dark background. Increasing light pollution to a Bortle scale 3 (bottom left) illustrates what a small town, suburban sky looks like. The brightest stars show through, and the Milky Way might just be barely visible. Increasing light pollution to a Bortle scale 9 (bottom right) illustrates what an inner-city night sky looks like. A couple of stars are all that's left in sight, and the Milky Way is no longer visible.*

If the amount of artificial light continues to grow unmitigated from the Flathead Valley to the south, the night sky view over Logan Pass will get pushed up the Bortle scale of light pollution.

Illustration 3. The night sky over Many Glacier and Mount Gould have been replaced with the sky chart from Stellarium. Clockwise from top left, we start with a high ISO photograph of the current night sky. The Bortle 1 illustration approximates this current condition. This represents an excellent dark sky location. A Bortle 3 location has lost some of the fainter stars, and this would represent a rural sky. Bortle 5 has lost most of the fainter stars, representing a suburban or small-town sky. In a Bortle 7 night sky, the Milky Way is lost as are most stars. And in a Bortle 9 night sky (far right), only a handful of the brightest stars are visible through the artificial glow.

If the amount of artificial light continues to increase from the Flathead Valley to the west, the night sky over Many Glacier will get pushed up the Bortle scale of light pollution, from the top left of this illustration towards the bottom right.

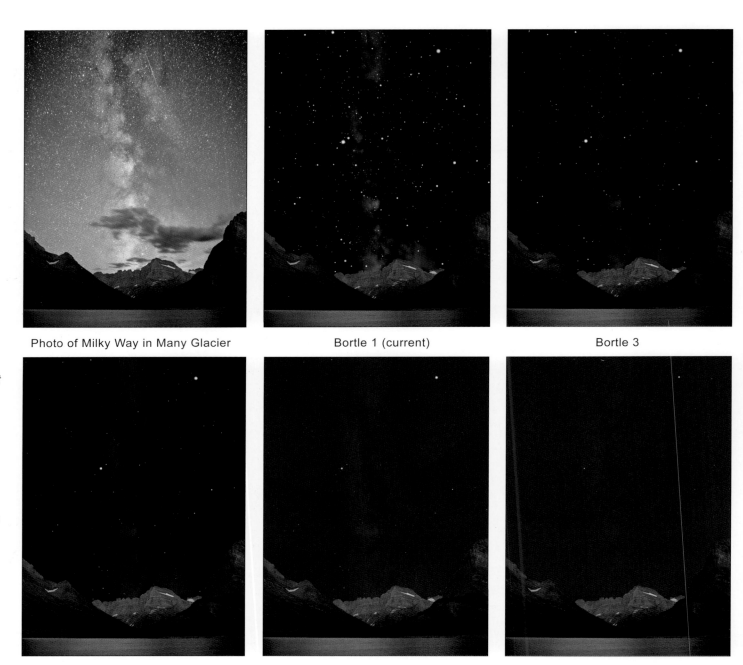

Photo of Milky Way in Many Glacier   Bortle 1 (current)   Bortle 3

Bortle 5   Bortle 7   Bortle 9

Illustration 4. *The midnight sky over Saint Mary Lake has been replaced with the sky chart from Stellarium. The far left column illustrates our current Bortle scale 1 night sky. Countless stars show on a dark background. Increasing light pollution to a Bortle scale 3 (second column) illustrates what a small town, suburban sky looks like. The brightest stars still show through. Increasing light pollution to a Bortle scale 9 (far right column) illustrates what an inner-city night sky looks like. Hardly any stars are visible.*

Currently, the real night sky already shows light from the Flathead Valley over Saint Mary Lake's western horizon.

BASICS OF DARK-SKY-FRIENDLY LIGHTING

Reclaiming the night sky will reconnect us to our ancestors, nurture our health, and remind us of our humble position within the cosmos. I wouldn't call it a bandwagon just yet, but the movement to control light pollution is quickly gaining momentum.

There are many websites devoted to the subject where you can find all of the nitty-gritty answers to specific questions that will eventually arise. But the most ground can be gained through just a handful of basic steps. See how many of the following simple suggestions might fit into your lifestyle. You might just find out how illuminating the night can be.

Reacquaint yourself with the night

Step one is to learn what a naturally dark sky is supposed to look like. Picking up this book is a good start. If dark landscapes aren't available where you live, then plan a trip. If you can't travel, then learn through photographs from dark places. You won't care about the night sky if you've never seen the real deal. Light pollution is insidious because it has become so pervasive that most of us don't realize what's been stolen from us.

For many people, the most interesting part of step one will be the exorcism of some ancient demons. To control people and create civil societies, early institutions of church and state demonized darkness to keep people indoors at night.[1] Darkness became analogous with danger, evil and immorality. This subliminal message remains deeply embedded in our subconscious minds — as if nothing dangerous, evil or immoral happens during the day.

Once you realize that darkness is not inherently bad, you will feel much less scared of the dark and you will open a whole new window for personal growth. Darkness is actually a good thing, and because of the way our brains are wired, quality darkness is absolutely essential for optimal health.

Use Light Appropriately

We could heal a major part of our light pollution ills if we just used our existing lights better. We often equate more light with better light, but we're actually just creating deeper shadows because of the way that our eyes' rods and cones work. We can do better.

Turn off unnecessary lights. Dim unnecessarily bright lights. Use motion sensors to turn lights on only when they are actually needed. Shield outdoor light fixtures so that light does not shine above the horizon and tresspass where it's not needed or wanted. Light buildings and monuments from the top down. Strive for zero uplighting, but if lights must point up, try to keep them within 45 degrees of the horizon.

Protect your health

We are chemically programmed for dark nights, and our health can suffer if we don't get enough true darkness. Fortunately, there are many things we can do at home to correct this modern problem.

Quality sleep is vital to good health. Make sure that your sleeping area is dark, as in *really dark*. Ideally, you should not be able to see your fingers when you wiggle your extended hand. Turn off any phones or computers in the room, as they emit the most damaging light wavelengths.

If you use a clock, look for one that projects a warm color, like red. Red light is least disruptive to your melatonin production at night. Use warm-colored night lights with motion sensors to find your way around if you need to get up and visit the facilities in the dark.

Avoid the blues — blue or white light bulbs. LEDs are great for energy conservation, but most current models emit the worst wavelengths. Look for LEDs that are 3000K or warmer.[2,3]

Lighting technology for electronic devices, like cell phones and computers, will improve as more people demand healthier light sources. The first generation of computer and phone applications are already here, and even better ones will no doubt follow. At present (2015), there are cell phone applications like Twilight and Lux that automatically dim your phone to match ambient light levels, and warm the phone's light colors to less damaging wavelengths. For your computer, there is the free software f.lux, which automatically dims and warms the monitor's color at night, and reduces the amount of blue light that you are exposed to (see *Resources* section).

Support region-wide dark sky efforts

Making personal changes to your relationship with artificial light is the place to start. Unfortunately, not everyone cares about good health — yours or theirs. So we also need to support minimum guidelines for region-wide control of artificial lighting because light pollution can trespass many miles from its source.

A handful of national parks that still have quality darkness are trying to raise public awareness by establishing dark sky preserves. But preserves can't prevent light trespass from the surrounding towns and communities. Currently, 16 states[3] and a number of municipalities have established lighting ordinances (including Kalispell, Whitefish and Missoula, MT). Tucson, Arizona — home of the International Dark Sky Association — instituted a lighting ordinance back in 1972. While Tucson's population has doubled In the last 20 years, its night sky brightness has actually decreased slightly over the same period.[4]

It can be done!

Hungry for more? The Dark Skies Awareness Project and Night Sky Network websites (next page) are chock full of excellent information. Welcome to the safer and healthier "dark side."

RESOURCES

Night Sky Preservation

Dark Skies Awareness Project (http://www.darkskiesawareness.org/faqs.php)

Dark Sky Approved Lighting Sources (http://www.darksky.org/ida-fixture-seal-of-approval/dark-sky-friendly-devices)

Dark Sky Society (http://www.darkskysociety.org/index.cfm)

Globe at Night (http://www.globeatnight.org/)

Good Neighbor Outdoor Lighting (http://stellafane.org/misc/images/gnol.pdf)

International Dark Sky Association (http://www.darksky.org/)

Jasper Dark Sky Preserve (http://jasperdarksky.org)

Light Pollution Abatement Site (http://calgary.rasc.ca/lp/index.html)

Light Pollution Atlas (N. America 2006) overlay in Google Maps (http://djlorenz.github.io/astronomy/lp2006/overlay/dark.html)

Light Pollution Interactive (http://www.globeatnight.org/light-pollution-interactive.php)

Light Pollution Science and Technology Institute (http://www.lightpollution.it/istil/index.html)

Night Sky National Park Programs (http://www.nightskyparks.org/)

Night Sky Network (http://nightsky.jpl.nasa.gov/index.cfm)

Starry Nights Light Fixtures (http://www.starrynightlights.com/)

Darkness and Human Health

f.lux, computer-dimming application. (https://justgetflux.com/)

Lux, cell phone dimming application. (http://www.vitocassisi.com/)

Twilight, cell phone dimming application. (https://sites.google.com/site/twilight4android/)

Astronomy

Astronomical Society of the Pacific (http://astrosociety.org/)

Astronomers Without Borders (http://www.astronomerswithoutborders.org/)

Blue Mountain Observatory, Missoula (http://cas.umt.edu/physics/Blue_Mountain_Observatory/)

CalSky Aurora Forecasts (https://www.calsky.com/cs.cgi/)

Canadian Space Agency (http://www.asc-csa.gc.ca/eng/default.asp)

Earth and Sky (http://earthsky.org/)

European Space Agency (http://www.esa.int/ESA)

Hubble Space Telescope (http://hubblesite.org/)

Live Comet Data (http://www.livecometdata.com/)

NASA Earth Observatory (http://earthobservatory.nasa.gov/)

NASA Science (http://science.nasa.gov/)

Royal Astronomy Society of Canada (http://www.rasc.ca/)

Soft Serve News Aurora forecasts (http://www.softservenews.com/)

Space (http://www.space.com/)

Space Weather (http://www.spaceweather.com/)

Stellarium Desktop Planetarium (http://www.stellarium.org/)

The Sky Live Planetarium (http://theskylive.com)

The World at Night (http://www.twanight.org/newTWAN/index.asp)

Universe Today (http://www.universetoday.com/)

Native Americans

Blackfoot Digital Library (http://blackfootdigitallibrary.com/)

Blackfeet Language Website (http://www.piikanipaitapiisin.com/)

Blackfeet Nation (http://www.blackfeetnation.com/)

Bullchild, Percy. *The Sun Came Down*. 1985. Harper & Row, San Francisco, CA. 390 pp.

Eggermont-Molenaar, Mary, ed. *Montana 1911: A professor and his wife among the Blackfeet.* 2005. Univ. of Calgary Press, AB. 417 pp.

Glacier Nat. Park Native Educational Materials (http://www.nps.gov/glac/forteachers/intro-to-native-american.htm)

Glenbow Museum (http://www.glenbow.org/blackfoot/)

Grinnell, G.B. *Blackfoot Lodge Tales*. 1892. Univ. of NE Press, Lincoln. 310 pp.

Hungry Wolf, Adolf. 2006. *The Blackfoot Papers - Volume Three: Pikunni Portfolio Glacier National Park*. Good Medicine Foundation.

Kainai–Blood Tribe (http://bloodtribe.org/)

Ktunaxa First Voices (http://www.firstvoices.com/en/Ktunaxa)

McClintock, Walter. *The Old North Trail*. 1910. Macmillan and Co. Londond, England.

Montana Indian Education for All (http://opi.mt.gov/Programs/IndianEd/Index.html)

Piegan Institute (http://www.pieganinstitute.org/)

Salish–Pend d'Oreille Culture Committee. 2005. *The Salish People and the Lewis and Clark Expedition*. Univ. of NE Press. 198pp.

Salish World (http://www.salishworld.com/)

Schultz, James.W. *My Life as an Indian*. 1907. Skyhorse Publishing, New York, NY. 426 pp.

Schultz, J.W. 1916. *Blackfeet Tales of Glacier National Park*. Riverbend Press, Helena, MT. 226 pp.

Schultz, J.W. 1930. *The Sun God's Children*. Riverbend Press, Helena, MT. 259 pp.

Wissler, Clark and D.C. Duvall. 1908. Mythology of the Blackfoot Indians. Univ. of NE Press, Lincoln. 166 pp.

Glacier/Waterton Region

Crown of the Continent (http://www.crownofthecontinent.net/index.php)

Flathead Watershed (http://www.flatheadwatershed.org/index.shtml)

Glacier National Park Conservancy (http://glacierconservancy.org)

Holterman, Jack. *Place Names of Glacier/Waterton National Parks*. 1985. Glacier Natural History Assoc. 169 pp.

NPS Glacier National Park (http://www.nps.gov/glac/index.htm)

Waterton Lakes National Park (http://www.pc.gc.ca/eng/pn-np/ab/waterton/index.aspx)

Photography

Cloudy Nights (http://www.cloudynights.com/page/index.html)

The Photographer's Ephemeris (http://photoephemeris.com/)

Books of Note

Anderson, Mark. *The Day the World Discovered the Sun*. 2012. Da Capo Press, Boston, MA. 280 pp.

Bryson, Bill. *A Short History of Nearly Everything*. 2003. Broadway Books, New York, NY. 544 pp.

Ekirch, A. Roger. *At Day's Close*. 2005. W.W. Norton & Company, New York, NY. 447 pp.

Ferris, Timothy. *Seeing in the Dark*. 2002. Simon & Schuster, New York, NY. 879 pp.

Ferris, T. *Coming of Age in the Milky Way*. 1988. Doubleday, New York, NY. 495 pp.

Graun, Ken. *What's Out Tonight?* 2007. Ken Press, Tuscon, AZ. 400 pp.

Krupp, E.C. *Beyond the Blue Horizon*. 1991. Harper Collins, New York, NY. 387 pp.

Longcore, Travis and Catherine Rich, eds. *Ecological Consequences of Artificial Night Lighting*. 2006. Island Press, Washington, DC. 459 pp.

(Websites current and active as of March 2015)

GLACIER NATIONAL PARK SKY EVENTS 2015–2024

2015

Jan 10 Mercury 0.6° of Venus at 18:00
Jan 20 Mars 1.5°S of Moon at 18:28
Mar 21 Mars 1.0°N of Moon at 15:13 (occultation)
Apr 22 Mercury 1.3° of Mars at 12:00
Apr 30 Mercury 1.6°S of Pleiades at 18:29
Jun 13 Venus 0.5°N of Beehive Cluster at 01:59
Jun 14 Mercury 0.0°N of Moon at 19:26 (occultation)
Jul 18 Venus 0.4°N of Moon at 18:06 (occultation)
Aug 07 Mercury 0.5° of Jupiter at 00:01
Aug 19 Mars 0.5°S of Beehive Cluster at 20:35
Oct 11 Mercury 1.0°N of Moon at 05:00 (occultation)
Nov 07 Mars 1.8°N of Moon at 02:56
Nov 07 Venus 1.2°N of Moon at 06:54
Dec 03 Jupiter 1.8°N of Moon at 23:21
Dec 05 Mars 0.1°N of Moon at 19:40 (occultation)
Dec 07 Venus 0.7°S of Moon at 09:55 (occultation)
Dec 31 Jupiter 1.5°N of Moon at 10:55

2016

Jan 03 Mars 1.5°S of Moon at 11:45
Jan 27 Jupiter 1.4°N of Moon at 18:14
Feb 23 Jupiter 1.7°N of Moon at 20:58
Apr 06 Venus 0.7°S of Moon at 01:30 (occultation)
Jun 03 Mercury 0.7o N of Moon at 02:47 (occultation)
Jun 11 Jupiter 1.5°N of Moon at 12:35
Jul 09 Jupiter 0.9°N of Moon at 03:08 (occultation)
Aug 04 Mercury 0.6°N of Moon at 15:12 (occultation)
Aug 05 Jupiter 0.2°N of Moon at 20:28 (occultation)
Sep 03 Venus 1.1°S of Moon at 03:33 (occultation)
Sep 29 Mercury 0.7°N of Moon at 03:42 (occultation)
Oct 28 Jupiter 1.4°S of Moon at 02:33
Nov 24 Jupiter 1.9°S of Moon at 18:47

2017

Jan 02 Venus 1.9°S of Moon at 02:20
Jan 02 Mars 0.2°S of Moon at 23:47 (occultation)
May 23 Mercury 1.6°N of Moon at 18:20
Jul 09 Mercury 0.1°N of Beehive Cluster at 18:33
July 25 Mercury 0.9° S of Moon at 01:49 (occultation)
Aug 31 Venus 1.4°S of Beehive Cluster at 23:08
Sep 16 Mercury 0.1° of Mars at 11:00
Sep 17 Venus 0.5°N of Moon at 17:56 (occultation)
Sep 18 Mercury 0.0°N of Moon at 16:22 (occultation)
Oct 17 Mars 1.8°S of Moon at 03:04
Dec 06 Mercury 1.3° of Saturn at 17:00

2018

Jan 13 Mercury 0.7° of Saturn at 01:00
Mar 03 Mercury 1.1° of Venus at 23:00
Apr 07 Saturn 1.9°S of Moon at 05:50
Apr 22 Beehive 1.9°N of Moon at 23:17

May 04 Saturn 1.7°S of Moon at 13:31
May 20 Beehive 1.7°N of Moon at 04:57
May 31 Saturn 1.6°S of Moon at 18:20
Jun 16 Beehive 1.5°N of Moon at 12:38
Jun 19 Venus 0.4°N of Beehive Cluster t 19:21
Jun 27 Saturn 1.8°S of Moon at 20:59
Jul 03 Mercury 0.6°S of Beehive Cluster at 20:39
Jul 15 Venus 1.6°S of Moon at 20:31
Sep 06 Beehive Cluster 1.4°N of Moon at 19:13
Oct 04 Beehive Cluster 1.3°N of Moon at 02:51
Oct 14 Saturn 1.8°S of Moon at 20:01
Oct 18 Mars 1.9°S of Moon at 06:01
Oct 31 Beehive 1.0°N of Moon at 08:24
Nov 11 Saturn 1.4°S of Moon at 08:46
Nov 15 Mars 1.0°N of Moon at 21:16 (occultation)
Nov 27 Beehive 0.8°N of Moon at 13:57
Dec 05 Mercury 1.9°S of Moon at 14:06
Dec 08 Saturn 1.1°S of Moon at 22:30 (occultation)
Dec 21 Mercury 0.8° of Jupiter at 13:00
Dec 24 Beehive 0.6°N of Moon at 21:52

2019

Jan 01 Venus 1.3°S of Moon at 14:50
Jan 21 Beehive 0.6°N of Moon at 08:32
Jan 31 Venus 0.1°S of Moon at 10:36 (occultation)
Feb 2 Saturn 0.6°S of Moon at 00:18 (occultation)
Feb 17 Beehive 0.6°N of Moon at 20:05
Mar 01 Saturn 0.3°S of Moon at 11:40 (occultation)
Mar 02 Venus 1.2°N of Moon at 14:28
Mar 17 Beehive 0.5°N of Moon at 06:01
Mar 28 Saturn 0.1°N of Moon at 22:11 (occultation)
Apr 13 Beehive 0.2°N of Moon at 13:12
Apr 23 Jupiter 1.6°S of Moon at 04:36
Apr 25 Saturn 0.4°N of Moon at 07:38 (occultation)
May 10 Beehive 0.0°S of Moon at 18:35
May 22 Saturn 0.5°N of Moon at 15:25 (occultation)
Jun 7 Beehive 0.2°S of Moon at 00:19
Jun 18 Mercury 0.2° of Mars at 11:00
Jun 18 Saturn 0.4°N of Moon at 20:58 (occultation)
Jul 04 Beehive 0.2°S of Moon at 08:02
Jul 13 Mars 0.4°S of Beehive at 00:06
Jul 16 Saturn 0.2°N of Moon at 00:27 (occultation)
Aug 12 Saturn 0.0°N of Moon at 03:05 (occultation)
Aug 16 Mercury 1.2°S of Beehive at 21:24
Aug 28 Beehive 0.2°S of Moon at 04:31
Sep 08 Saturn 0.0°N of Moon at 06:53 (occultation)
Sep 24 Beehive 0.4°S of Moon at 14:15
Oct 05 Saturn 0.3°N of Moon at 13:48 (occultation)
Oct 21 Beehive 0.6°S of Moon at 21:41
Oct 31 Jupiter 1.3°S of Moon at 07:22
Nov 18 Beehive 0.9°S of Moon at 03:11
Nov 28 Jupiter 0.7°S of Moon at 03:49 (occultation)
Nov 29 Saturn 0.9°N of Moon at 14:12 (occultation)
Dec 15 Beehive 1.0°S of Moon at 08:54
Dec 28 Venus 1.0°N of Moon at 18:32 (occultation)

2020

Jan 11 Beehive 1.0°S of Moon at 16:54
Jan 22 Jupiter 0.4°N of Moon at 19:42 (occultation)
Feb 08 Beehive 1.0°S of Moon at 03:16
Feb 18 Mars 0.8°S of Moon at 06:18 (occultation)
Feb 19 Jupiter 0.9°N of Moon at 12:36 (occultation)
Feb 06 Beehive 1.1°S of Moon at 14:18
Feb 18 Mars 0.7°N of Moon at 01:18 (occultation)
Feb 18 Jupiter 1.5°N of Moon at 03:18
Apr 02 Beehive 1.3°S of Moon at 23:25
Apr 03 Venus 0.3°S of Pleiades at 07:36
May 22 Mercury 0.9° of Venus at 03:00
May 27 Beehive 1.7°S of Moon at 11:44
Jun 19 Venus 0.7°S of Moon at 01:52 (occultation)
Aug 01 Jupiter 1.5°N of Moon at 16:30
Aug 09 Mars 0.8°N of Moon at 00:57 (occultation)
Aug 28 Jupiter 1.4°N of Moon at 18:33
Sep 05 Mars 0.0°S of Moon at 21:42 (occultation)
Sep 24 Jupiter 1.6°N of Moon at 23:46
Oct 02 Mars 0.7°N of Moon at 20:21 (occultation)
Dec 12 Venus 0.8°S of Moon at 13:40 (occultation)

2021

Jan 09 Mercury 1.6° of Saturn at 22:00
Jan 11 Mercury 1.4° of Jupiter at 11:00
Jan 11 Venus 1.5°N of Moon at 13:12
Mar 04 Mercury 0.3° of Jupiter at 22:00
Mar 17 Mars 0.1°N of Moon at 05:09 (occultation)
May 15 Mars 1.5°S of Moon at 21:47
May 28 Mercury 0.4° of Venus at 20:00
Jun 11 Venus 1.5°S of Moon at 23:44
Jun 22 Mars 0.3°S of Beehive at 22:21
Jul 02 Venus 0.1°N of Beehive at 19:45
Aug 18 Mercury 0.1° of Mars at 20:00
Nov 03 Mercury 1.2°S of Moon at 11:40 (occultation)
Nov 07 Venus 1.1°S of Moon at 22:21 (occultation)
Dec 31 Mars 1.0°N of Moon at 13:13 (occultation)

2022

Mar 02 Mercury 0.7° of Saturn at 09:00
Mar 20 Mercury 1.2° of Jupiter at 23:00
Apr 29 Mercury 1.3°S of Pleiades at 12:31
May 26 Venus 0.2°N of Moon at 19:52 (occultation)
Jun 22 Mars 0.9°N of Moon at 11:16 (occultation)
Jul 21 Mars 1.1°S of Moon at 09:46 (occultation)
Aug 17 Venus 0.9°S of Beehive at 09:02
Sep 11 Jupiter 1.8°N of Moon at 08:11
Dec 07 Mars 0.5°S of Moon at 21:21 (occultation)
Dec 29 Mercury 1.4° of Venus at 00:01

2023

Jan 03 Mars 0.5°N of Moon at 12:35 (occultation)

Jan 25 Jupiter 1.8°N of Moon at 19:00
Jan 30 Mars 0.1°N of Moon at 21:24 (occultation)
Feb 22 Jupiter 1.2°N of Moon at 14:58 (occultation)
Feb 27 Mars 1.1°S of Moon at 21:32 (occultation)
Mar 02 Mercury 0.9° of Saturn at 07:00
Mar 24 Venus 0.1°N of Moon at 03:28 (occultation)
Mar 25 Pleiades 1.9°N of Moon at 16:42
Apr 23 Venus 1.3°S of Moon at 06:03
May 17 Jupiter 0.8°S of Moon at 06:15 (occultation)
Jun 01 Mars 0.1°S of Moon at 20:35
Jun 13 Venus 0.5°N of Beehive at 04:05
Jun 13 Jupiter 1.5°S of Moon at 23:33
Jun 15 Pleiades 1.8°N of Moon at 17:47
Jul 12 23:31 Pleiades 1.7°N of Moon
Jul 14 Mercury 0.2°N of Beehive at 15:33
Aug 09 Pleiades 1.5°N of Moon at 05:06
Oct 02 Pleiades 1.1°N of Moon at 21:25
Oct 30 Pleiades 1.1°N of Moon at 07:30
Nov 09 Venus 1.0°S of Moon at 02:28 (occultation)
Nov 26 Pleiades 1.1°N of Moon at 17:02
Dec 24 Pleiades 1.1°N of Moon at 00:37

2024

Jan 20 Pleiades 0.9°N of Moon at 06:25
Jan 27 Mercury 0.2° of Mars at 09:00
Feb 16 Pleiades 0.6°N of Moon at 12:13
Mar 14 Pleiades 0.4°N of Moon at 19:54
Apr 06 Saturn 1.2°N of Moon at 02:20 (occultation)
Apr 07 Venus 0.4°S of Moon at 09:39 (occultation)
Apr 11 Pleiades 0.4°N of Moon at 05:38
Apr 19 Mercury 1.7° of Venus at 06:00
May 03 Saturn 0.8°N of Moon at 15:26 (occultation)
May 04 Mars 0.2°S of Moon at 19:26(occultation)
May 31 Saturn 0.4°N of Moon at 01:01(occultation)
Jun 04 Mercury 0.1° of Jupiter at 03:00
Jun 27 Saturn 0.1°S of Moon at 07:52 (occultation)
Jul 02 Pleiades 0.3°N of Moon at 08:30
Jul 06 Mercury 0.1°S of Beehive Cluster at 14:12
Jul 24 Saturn 0.4°S of Moon at 13:38 (occultation)
Jul 29 Pleiades 0.1°N of Moon at 14:13
Aug 05 Venus 1.7°S of Moon at 15:04
Aug 20 Saturn 0.4°S of Moon at 19:54 (occultation)
Aug 25 Pleiades 0.1°S of Moon at 19:54
Sep 05 Venus 1.2°N of Moon at 03:03
Sep 17 Saturn 0.3°S of Moon at 03:14 (occultation)
Sep 22 Pleiades 0.2°S of Moon at 03:17
Oct 14 Saturn 0.1°S of Moon at 11:05 (occultation)
Oct 19 Pleiades 0.1°S of Moon at 12:59
Nov 10 Saturn 0.1°S of Moon at 18:36 (occultation)
Nov 15 Pleiades 0.1°S of Moon at 23:59
Dec 03 Mars 1.3°N of Beehive Cluster at 07:03
Dec 08 Saturn 0.3°S of Moon at 01:39 (occultation)
Dec 13 Pleiades 0.1°S of Moon at 10:13
Dec 18 Mars 0.9°S of Moon at 01:36 (occultation)

Table 1. Select moon, planet and star cluster conjunctions (near passes) of less than two degrees, and Moon and planetary occultations (eclipses). Mountain Standard times given, add one hour during daylight savings time. Data from many public sources (mostly NASA) and from www.AstroPixels.com courtesy of Goddard Scientist Emeritus, Fred Espenak.

Year	New Moon	Full Moon	Solstice/Equinox	Eclipse	MeteorShowers, peak (begin-end)
2015	Jan 20, Feb 18, Mar 20, Apr 18, May 17, Jun 16, Jul 15, Aug 14, Sep 12, Oct 12, Nov 11, Dec 11	Feb 3, Mar 5, Apr 4, May 3, Jun 2, Jul 1, Jul 31, Aug 29, Sep 27, Oct 27, Nov 25, Dec 25	Spring Equinox Mar 20; Summer Solstice Jun 21; Fall Equinox Sep 23; Winter Solstice Dec 22	Apr 4 Lunar Total 02:01-07:59; 27 Sep Lunar Total 17:12-22:22	Quadrantid, Jan 3-4 (Jan 1-10); Lyrid, Apr 22-23 (Apr 16-25); Eta-Aquarid, May 6-7 (Apr 19 - May 26); Alpha Capricornid Jul 27-28 (Jul 11- Aug 10); Delta-Aquarid, Jul 28-29 (Jul 21- Aug 23); Perseid, Aug 12-13 (Jul 13 - Aug 26); Orionid, Oct 21-22 (Oct 4 - Nov 14); S. Taurid, Oct 23-24 (Sep 7 - Nov 19); N. Taurid, Nov 11-12 (Oct 19 - Dec 10); Leonid, Nov 17-18 (Nov 5-30); Geminid, Dec 13-14 (Dec 4-16); Ursid, Dec 21-22 (Dec 17-23)
2016	Jan 9, Feb 8, Mar 8, Apr 7, May 6, Jun 4, Jul 4, Aug 2, Sep 1, Sep 30, Oct 30, Nov 29, Dec 28	Jan 23, Feb 22, Mar 23, Apr 21, May 21, Jun 20, Jul 19, Aug 18, Sep 16, Oct 15, Nov 14, Dec 13	Spring Equinox Mar 20; Summer Solstice Jun 20; Fall Equinox Sep 23; Winter Solstice Dec 21	Mar 23 Lunar Penumbral 02:39-06:55	Quadrantid, Jan 3-4 (Jan 1-10); Lyrid, Apr 22-23 (Apr 16-25); Eta-Aquarid, May 6-7 (Apr 19 - May 26); Alpha Capricornid Jul 27-28 (Jul 11- Aug 10); Delta-Aquarid, Jul 28-29 (Jul 21- Aug 23); Perseid, Aug 12-13 (Jul 13 - Aug 26); Orionid, Oct 21-22 (Oct 4 - Nov 14); S. Taurid, Oct 23-24 (Sep 7 - Nov 19); N. Taurid, Nov 11-12 (Oct 19 - Dec 10); Leonid, Nov 17-18 (Nov 5-30); Geminid Dec 13-14 (Dec 4-16); Ursid, Dec 21-22 (Dec 17-23)
2017	Jan 27, Feb 26, Mar 27, Apr 26, May 25, Jun 23, Jul 23, Aug 21, Sep 19, Oct 19, Nov 18, Dec 17	Jan 12, Feb 10, Mar 12, Apr 10, May 10, Jun 9, Jul 8, Aug 7, Sep 6, Oct 5, Nov 3, Dec 3	Spring Equinox Mar 20; Summer Solstice Jun 21; Fall Equinox Sep 22; Winter Solstice Dec 21	Feb 10 Lunar Penumbral 15:34-19:53; 21 Aug 85% Solar Partial 09:17-11:50	Quadrantid, Jan 3-4 (Jan 1-10); Lyrid, Apr 22-23 (Apr 16-25); Eta-Aquarid, May 6-7 (Apr 19 - May 26); Alpha Capricornid Jul 27-28 (Jul 11- Aug 10); Delta-Aquarid, Jul 28-29 (Jul 21- Aug 23); Perseid, Aug 12-13 (Jul 13 - Aug 26); Orionid, Oct 21-22 (Oct 4 - Nov 14); S. Taurid, Oct 23-24 (Sep 7 - Nov 19); N. Taurid, Nov 11-12 (Oct 19 - Dec 10); Leonid, Nov 17-18 (Nov 5-30); Geminid, Dec 13-14 (Dec 4-16); Ursid, Dec 21-22 (Dec 17-23)
2018	Jan 16, Feb 16, Mar 17, Apr 15, May 15, Jun 13, Jul 12, Aug 11, Sep 9, Oct 8, Nov 7, Dec 7	Jan 1, Jan 31, Mar 1, Mar 31, Apr 29, May 29, Jun 27, Jul 27, Aug 26, Sep 24, Oct 24, Nov 22, Dec 22	Spring Equinox Mar 20; Summer Solstice Jun 21; Fall Equinox Sep 23; Winter Solstice Dec 21	Jan 31 Lunar Total 03:51-09:08	Quadrantid, Jan 3-4 (Jan 1-10); Lyrid, Apr 22-23 (Apr 16-25); Eta-Aquarid, May 6-7 (Apr 19 - May 26); Alpha Capricornid Jul 27-28 (Jul 11- Aug 10); Delta-Aquarid, Jul 28-29 (Jul 21- Aug 23); Perseid, Aug 12-13 (Jul 13 - Aug 26); Orionid, Oct 21-22 (Oct 4 - Nov 14); S. Taurid, Oct 23-24 (Sep 7 - Nov 19); N. Taurid, Nov 11-12 (Oct 19 - Dec 10); Leonid, Nov 17-18 (Nov 5-30); Geminid, Dec 13-14 (Dec 4-16); Ursid, Dec 21-22 (Dec 17-23)
2019	Jan 5, Feb 4, Mar 6, Apr 5, May 4, Jun 3, Jul 2, Jul 31, Aug 30, Sep 28, Oct 27, Nov 26, Dec 25	Jan 20, Feb 19, Mar 20, Apr 19, May 18, Jun 17, Jul 16, Aug 15, Sep 13, Oct 13, Nov 12, Dec 11	Spring Equinox Mar 20; Summer Solstice Jun 21; Fall Equinox Sep 23; Winter Solstice Dec22	Jan 20 Lunar Total 19:37-00:48	Quadrantid, Jan 3-4 (Jan 1-10); Lyrid, Apr 22-23 (Apr 16-25); Eta-Aquarid, May 6-7 (Apr 19 - May 26); Alpha Capricornid Jul 27-28 (Jul 11- Aug 10); Delta-Aquarid, Jul 28-29 (Jul 21- Aug 23); Perseid, Aug 12-13 (Jul 13 - Aug 26); Orionid, Oct 21-22 (Oct 4 - Nov 14); S. Taurid, Oct 23-24 (Sep 7 - Nov 19); N. Taurid, Nov 11-12 (Oct 19 - Dec 10); Leonid, Nov 17-18 (Nov 5-30); Geminid, Dec 13-14 (Dec 4-16); Ursid, Dec 21-22 (Dec 17-23)
2020	Jan 24, Feb 23, Mar 24, Apr 22, May 22, Jun 20, Jul 20, Aug 18, Sep 17, Oct 16, Nov 14, Dec 14	Jan 10, Feb 9, Mar 9, Apr 7, May 7, Jun 5, Jul 4, Aug 3, Sep 1, Oct 1, Oct 31, Nov 30, Dec 29	Spring Equinox Mar 20; Summer Solstice Jun 20; Fall Equinox Sep 22; Winter Solstice Dec 21	July 4 Lunar Penumbral 20:07-22:52; Nov 30 Lunar Penumbral 00:32-04:53	Quadrantid, Jan 3-4 (Jan 1-10); Lyrid, Apr 22-23 (Apr 16-25); Eta-Aquarid, May 6-7 (Apr 19 - May 26); Alpha Capricornid Jul 27-28 (Jul 11- Aug 10); Delta-Aquarid, Jul 28-29 (Jul 21- Aug 23); Perseid, Aug 12-13 (Jul 13 - Aug 26); Orionid, Oct 21-22 (Oct 4 - Nov 14); S. Taurid, Oct 23-24 (Sep 7 - Nov 19); N. Taurid, Nov 11-12 (Oct 19 - Dec 10); Leonid, Nov 17-18 (Nov 5-30); Geminid, Dec 13-14 (Dec 4-16); Ursid, Dec 21-22 (Dec 17-23)
2021	Jan 12, Feb 11, Mar 13, Apr 11, May 11, Jun 10, Jul 9, Aug 8, Sep 6, Oct 6, Nov 4, Dec 4	Jan 1, Feb 27, Mar 28, Apr 26, May 26, Jun 24, Jul 23, Aug 22, Sep 20, Oct 20, Nov 19, Dec 18	Spring Equinox Mar 20; Summer Solstice Jun 21; Fall Equinox Sep 22; Winter Solstice Dec 21	May 26 Lunar Total 01:48-06:50; Nov 18-19 Lunar Partial 23:02-05:04	Quadrantid, Jan 3-4 (Jan 1-10); Lyrid, Apr 22-23 (Apr 16-25); Eta-Aquarid, May 6-7 (Apr 19 - May 26); Alpha Capricornid Jul 27-28 (Jul 11- Aug 10); Delta-Aquarid, Jul 28-29 (Jul 21- Aug 23); Perseid, Aug 12-13 (Jul 13 - Aug 26); Orionid, Oct 21-22 (Oct 4 - Nov 14); S. Taurid, Oct 23-24 (Sep 7 - Nov 19); N. Taurid, Nov 11-12 (Oct 19 - Dec 10); Leonid, Nov 17-18 (Nov 5-30); Geminid, Dec 13-14 (Dec 4-16); Ursid, Dec 21-22 (Dec 17-23)
2022	Jan 2, Jan 31, Mar 2, Mar 31, Apr 30, May 30, Jun 28, July 28, Aug 27, Sep 25, Oct 25, Nov 23, Dec 23	Jan 17, Feb 16, Mar 18, Apr 16, May 15, Jun 14, Jul 13, Aug 11, Sep 10, Oct 9, Nov 8, Dec 7	Spring Equinox Mar 20; Summer Solstice Jun 21; Fall Equinox Sep 23; Winter Solstice Dec 21	May 15 Lunar Total 18:32-23:51; Nov 8 Lunar Total 01:02-06:56	Quadrantid, Jan 3-4 (Jan 1-10); Lyrid, Apr 22-23 (Apr 16-25); Eta-Aquarid, May 6-7 (Apr 19 - May 26); Alpha Capricornid Jul 27-28 (Jul 11- Aug 10); Delta-Aquarid, Jul 28-29 (Jul 21- Aug 23); Perseid, Aug 12-13 (Jul 13 - Aug 26); Orionid, Oct 21-22 (Oct 4 - Nov 14); S. Taurid, Oct 23-24 (Sep 7 - Nov 19); N. Taurid, Nov 11-12 (Oct 19 - Dec 10); Leonid, Nov 17-18 (Nov 5-30); Geminid, Dec 13-14 (Dec 4-16); Ursid, Dec 21-22 (Dec 17-23)
2023	Jan 21, Feb 20, Mar 21, Apr 19, May 19, Jun 17, Jul 17, Aug 16, Sep 14, Oct 14, Nov 13, Dec 12	Jan 6, Feb 5, Mar 7, Apr 5, May 5, Jun 3, Jul 3, Aug 1, Aug 30, Sep 29, Oct 28, Nov 27, Dec 26	Spring Equinox Mar 20; Summer Solstice Jun 21; Fall Equinox Sep 23; Winter Solstice Dec 22	14 Oct 68% Solar Partial 08:11-10:46	Quadrantid, Jan 3-4 (Jan 1-10); Lyrid, Apr 22-23 (Apr 16-25); Eta-Aquarid, May 6-7 (Apr 19 - May 26); Alpha Capricornid Jul 27-28 (Jul 11- Aug 10); Delta-Aquarid, Jul 28-29 (Jul 21- Aug 23); Perseid, Aug 12-13 (Jul 13 - Aug 26); Orionid, Oct 21-22 (Oct 4 - Nov 14); S. Taurid, Oct 23-24 (Sep 7 - Nov 19); N. Taurid, Nov 11-12 (Oct 19 - Dec 10); Leonid, Nov 17-18 (Nov 5-30); Geminid, Dec 13-14 (Dec 4-16); Ursid, Dec 21-22 (Dec 17-23)
2024	Jan 11, Feb 9, Mar 10, Apr 8, May 7, Jun 6, July 5, Aug 4, Sep 2, Oct 2, Nov 1, Nov 30, Dec 30	Jan 25, Feb 24, Mar 25, Apr 23, May 23, Jun 21, Jul 21, Aug 19, Sep 17, Oct 17, Nov 15, Dec 15	Spring Equinox Mar 20; Summer Solstice Jun 20; Fall Equinox Sep 22; Winter Solstice Dec 21	Mar 24-25 Lunar Partial 21:53-2:32; 8 Apr 29% Solar Partial 10:43-12:37; Sep 17 Lunar Partial 17:41-21:47	Quadrantid, Jan 3-4 (Jan 1-10); Lyrid, Apr 22-23 (Apr 16-25); Eta-Aquarid, May 6-7 (Apr 19 - May 26); Alpha Capricornid Jul 27-28 (Jul 11- Aug 10); Delta-Aquarid, Jul 28-29 (Jul 21- Aug 23); Perseid, Aug 12-13 (Jul 13 - Aug 26); Orionid, Oct 21-22 (Oct 4 - Nov 14); S. Taurid, Oct 23-24 (Sep 7 - Nov 19); N. Taurid, Nov 11-12 (Oct 19 - Dec 10); Leonid, Nov 17-18 (Nov 5-30); Geminid, Dec 13-14 (Dec 4-16); Ursid, Dec 21-22 (Dec 17-23)

Table 2. Year-at-a-glance major sky events for Glacier National Park. Local eclipse times and percentages are calculated for Apgar Visitor's Center.

A SHOT IN THE DARK

Camera in one hand, flashlight in the other. Bouncing somewhere behind me is a dim headlamp that fell off when I started running. My flashlight occasionally spots a rather portly porcupine who's covering a surprising amount of ground at a dead sprint.

I didn't know porcupines could run so dang fast. Slowly gaining on him, I circle around and begin herding this fellow back towards my car, left idling there in the middle of a muddy road with the driver's door still open. We both stop, both of us panting. It's 3:08 a.m., the temperature dangling a few degrees above freezing.

We size each other up in the middle of nowhere, Montana, just a few miles east of Glacier National Park. Out here it's wheat stubble as far as the eye can see, in the glow of September's Harvest Moon. I stop to wonder, is this job normal? This porcupine was just the first of three well-armed critters that I encounter on my job before the night surrenders to dawn.

~ ~ ~

I previously scouted at least five locations for chasing the Harvest Moon's rise and set. I headed out into the night, south around Glacier, east across the Continental Divide, through the slumbering Blackfeet Nation, then north almost to Canada again before finally turning towards the park.

Humming pavement gave way to gravel, which turned to mud just a few miles before the so-called road vanished in the middle of a rutted wheat field. Google Earth lied to me — you can't get there from here without a helicopter. It's 4:15 a.m., still time for a plan B before moonset at sunrise. I turned the car around ever so carefully, so not to end up stuck where no one had driven for decades.

Within two minutes, headlights appeared on my previously deserted road. A white truck with a green stripe passed in the opposite direction, then spun around to follow close behind. Calling in my license plate, I figured. I pulled over, and he turned on his flashing red and blue lights. I knew what was happening, but he didn't, so I rested both empty hands in my open window in plain sight. No need for extra testosterone right now.

"What are you doin' out here?" His demeanor was polite, more than just a little curious.

"Tryin' not to get stuck. Did I wake you up, or are you on duty all night?" Officer Paycheck said he was on all night. He excused himself to walk back so I wouldn't hear his radio traffic, then returned.

"You the registered owner of this vehicle? Yeah, there's a road but it's barely a two-track. I wouldn't try it myself. You carrying any weapons?"

He steps backs again, but I can hear the radio crackle, "...be advised, no wants or warrants for that individual." My turn to ask a question.

"You ever see porcupines out here?" I had clocked it — three miles from the panting porcupine to the nearest tree (porcupines mostly eat the cambium layer under tree bark).

"Yeah, they're all over the place," he told me. This is a really strange place, I thought.

Another border patrol agent pulls up. Back-up for some strange guy muttering about porcupines. I explained that I wanted to photograph the mountains from further away, not closer — making the moon look bigger — but they didn't seem to understand. Both were chuckling at me now.

"Glad I could make your morning more interesting," I said. "I'll head back to the mountains. If I get a decent photo tonight you can see it on my website."

"What's your website address?" asked Officer Paycheck, now my newest friend.

"It's my name dot com," I told him. He asked again how to spell my name. "Don't worry," I said, "dispatch wrote it down." Something about me always leaves border patrol officers laughing. Still, I didn't have the courage to ask the agents if I could take their picture in the moonlight.

~ ~ ~

This was one of those rare summer nights. Not only was the sky clear above Lake McDonald, but my wife, Tracy, was joining me tonight while I made a star trails image. It finally grew dark enough at 12:20 a.m., and I started my cameras.

We laid back on Apgar's pebble beach to watch for shooting stars and listen to deer walking in the grass nearby. Otherwise, all was silent.

At 2:14 a.m. sharp, a guitar started playing softly not 50 yards down the beach. We couldn't see anything. Someone started singing Jack Johnson's "Better Together." I immediately turned to Tracy, "I planned that."

~ ~ ~

I met a polite park ranger one night in 1987, after I had parked my car along the east shore of Lake McDonald to photograph star trails overnight. Twenty-six years later, I was back on the same dark shore waiting for a comet to rise above the horizon.

After a couple of hours of fruitlessly scanning and second-guessing my calculations, I heard a car heading up from Apgar in the middle of the night. It pulled in behind mine and, a minute later, the headlights and engine turned off. His door closed softly. He was checking the hood to see if I'd been parked long enough for the engine to cool off.

I was kind of hoping that the park ranger would run the license plate, recognize my name, and be on his way. Then I remembered the car was registered in my wife's name. So I turned on my red headlamp and stumbled 50 yards down the rocky beach before cutting up the social trail leading uphill through cedar trees to the pullout. I was just about to clear the trees when suddenly, the spotlight.

"Aaarrggh! You're blinding me, turn that flashlight off! Mark, it's me, John Ashley."

I'm not camping, I explained, just standing on the lake shore and photographing stars. As my vision started to recover, I noticed the ranger's short brown hair was now gray. I hardly recognized him, and he had forgotten me over all these years.

Source Notes

Prologue

1–3. P. Cinzano et al. 2001. *The first World Atlas of the artificial night sky brightness.* Monthly Notices of the Royal Astronomical Society 328, 689–707. (http://www.lightpollution.it/cinzano/download/0108052.pdf)

4. Parks Canada. 2008. *Guidelines and Specifications for Outdoor Lighting at Parks Canada.* Prepared by the Real Property and Ecological Integrity Branches of Parks Canada. 25 pp.

5. The Glacier Park Conservancy. 2014. *Half the Park Happens After Dark,* in *The 2015 field guide to park project priorities.* 40 pp.

Sky Stories

1. Glenbow Museum virtual exhibit, *Niitsitapiisini, The Story of the Blackfoot People.* Calgary, Alberta. (http://www.glenbow.org/blackfoot/EN/html/index.htm)

2. Tovias, Blanca. 2001. *Colonialism on the Prairies: Blackfoot Settlement and Cultural Transformation, 1870–1920 (First Nations and the Colonial Encounter).* Brighton, England. Sussex Academic Press. 307 pp.

3. See: The Piegan Institute. Browning, MT (http://www.pieganinstitute.org/). Nkwusm Salish School. Arlee, MT (http://www.salishworld.com/). White Clay Immersion School. Harlem, MT (no website). Kalispel Tribe of Indians. Usk, WA (http://kalispeltribe.com/our-tribe/language).

4. Blackfoot Crossing Historical Park. Siksika, Alberta. (http://www.blackfootcrossing.ca/storyrobes.html)

5–7. Tovias, Blanca. 2001.

8. Chamberlain, V. 1984. *Astronomical content of North American Plains Indian calendars.* In *Archaeoastronomy* (U.K.), No. 6, p. S1 - S54. (http://adsabs.harvard.edu/full/1984JHAS...15....1C)

Also see: Dempsy, Hugh A. *A Blackfoot Winter Count.* 1965. Paper written by Glenbow Foundation archivist. Calgary, Alberta. (http://www.telusplanet.net/public/mtoll/winter.htm).

9. Canadian Heritage Information Network. 2003. *Indigenous Astronomy: The Blackfoot of The North American Plains. The Sky Beings (The Moon, Sun and Morning Star - The Planet Venus).* (http://www.museevirtuel.ca/edu/ViewLoitDa.do;jsessionid=A985C0?method=preview&lang =EN&id=5216)

Also see: Vest, Jay Hansford. 1988. *Traditional Blackfeet Religion and the Sacred Badger-Two Medicine Wildlands.* Journal of Law and Religion, Vol. 6, No. 2 (1988), pp. 455-489.

10. Bullchild, Percy. 1985. *The Sun Came Down. The History of the World as My Blackfeet Elders Told It.* Harper & Row. San Francisco, CA. 390 pp.

11. Glenbow Museum virtual exhibit, *Niitsitapiisini, The Story of the Blackfoot People.* Calgary, Alberta. (http://www.glenbow.org/blackfoot/EN/html/evening.htm)

12. Gladstone, Jack. 2015. Pers. com.

Going-to-the-Sun ~ Staying for the Stars

1. Cally, Paul. 2014. *Giant sunspot returns – and it's bigger and badder than ever.* Physics.org (http://phys.org/news/2014-11-giant-sunspot-bigger-badder.html)

2. Burnett, Jim. 2007. *Hey Ranger 2.* Taylor Trade Publishing. Washington, DC. 270 pp.

3. Sharp, Tim. 2012. *How Big is the Sun? | Size of the Sun.* Space.com (http://www.space.com/17001-how-big-is-the-sun-size-of-the-sun.html)

4. EarthSky.org. 2014. *How many stars can you see on a clear, moonless night?* (http://earthsky.org/space/how-many-stars-could-you-see-on-a-clear-moonless-night)

5. Herman, Rhett. 1998. *How fast is the earth moving?* Scientific American. (http://www.scientificamerican.com/article/how-fast-is-the-earth-mov/)

6. Platt, Phil. 1999. *Twinkle Twinkle Little Star.* BadAstronomy.com (http://www.badastronomy.com/bitesize/twinkle.html)

7–8. Schultz, Colin. 2014. *The Surprisingly Complicated Reason Why Stars Look Like They Have Points.* Smithsonian.com (http://www.smithsonianmag.com/smart-news/surprisingly-complicated-reason-why-stars-seem-have-points-180952587/?no-ist)

Sunset, Alpenglow, Twilight & the Golden Hour

1. Natl. Weather Service. Undated. *Three Types of Twilight.* (http://www.crh.noaa.gov/lmk/?n=twilight-types)

2. Moffatt, Roger. Undated. *The Golden Hour Calculator.* (http://www.golden-hour.com/)

3. Holterman, Jack. 1985. *Place Names of Glacier/Waterton National Parks,* pp. 94, 138. Glacier Natural History Assoc., West Glacier, MT. 169 pp.

4. Holterman, Jack. 1985. Page 110.

5. Holterman, Jack. 1985. Page 66.

6. Holterman, Jack. 1985. Page 137.

The Belt of Venus

1–2. Nave, Carl R. 2012. *Blue Sky and Rayleigh Scattering.* HyperPhysics.edu, GA State Univ., Atlanta. (http://hyperphysics.phy-astr.gsu.edu/hbase/atmos/blusky.html#c3)

3. Institute of Physics. Undated. *Why is the Sky Blue,* on Physics.org. London, England. (http://www.physics.org/article-questions.asp?id=108)

4. Greenler, Robert. 1990. *Rainbows, Halos and Glories,* pp. 131-132. Cambridge Univ. Press, MA. 205 pp.

5. Flanders, Tony. 2010. *The Belt of Venus,* in Sky & Telescope. (http://www.skyandtelescope.com/astronomy-blogs/the-belt-of-venus/)

6. Schultz, James W. 1926. *Signposts of Adventure: Glacier National Park as the Indians Know it.* Houghton Mifflin Co., Boston, MA. 224 pp.

Moonrise in the Mountains

1. Wissler, Clark, and D.C. Duvall. 2007. *The Moon Woman,* pp. 72-73 in, *Mythology of the Blackfoot Indians,* 2nd Edition. Univ. of NE Press. Lincoln, NE. 167 pp.

Old Chief ~ Governor of the Mountains

1. Natl. Park Service. 2006. *Ninaistako (Chief Mountain).* Crown of the Continent Research Learning Center Resource Bulletin. 2 pp.

2. Clark, Ella Elizabeth. 1960. *The white horses on Chief Mountain,* in *Indian Legends of Canada.* McClelland & Stewart, Inc. Toronto, Ontario. 177 pp.

3. MacGregor, J. G. 1966. *Peter Fidler, Canada's Forgotten Explorer 1769-1822.* Fifth House, Ltd., Calgary, AB. 265 pp.

4. Lavender, David. 2001. *Chapter 2,* in *The Journals of the Lewis and Clark Expedition.* Undated. (http://lewisandclarkjournals.unl.edu/read/?_xmlsrc=lc.lavender.01.02&_xslsrc=LCstyles.xsl)

5. Fidler, Peter. Unpublished journal. *Journal of a Journey over Land from Buckingham House to the Rocky Mountains in 1792-93.* (http://www.ourheritage.net/index_page_stuff/following_trails/fidler/Fidler2.html)

6. Lewis, Meriwether. Wednesday June 5th 1805 *The Journals of the Lewis and Clark Expedition.* (http://lewisandclarkjournals.unl.edu/read/?_xmlsrc=1805-06-05&_xslsrc=LCstyles.xsl)

7. Lavender, David. 2001.

8. Lewis, Meriwether. Tuesday July 22ed 1806. *The Journals of the Lewis and Clark Expedition.* (http://lewisandclarkjournals.unl.edu/read/?_xmlsrc=1806-07-22.xml&_xslsrc=LCstyles.xsl)

Lunar Attractions

1–2. NASA. *GRAIL and the mystery of the missing moon.* 2011, in NASA Science News. (http://science.nasa.gov/science-news/science-at-nasa/2011/07sep_twomoons/)

3. Chu, Jennifer. 2013. *An answer to a lunar mystery: Why is the moon's gravity so uneven?* MIT News Office. MIT News website. (http://newsoffice.mit.edu/2013/an-answer-to-why-lunar-gravity-is-so-uneven-0530)

4. Cain, Frasier. 2012. *The Moon.* Universe Today website (http://www.universetoday.com/19424/the-moon/)

5. Steigerwald, Bill. 2012. *Researchers Estimate Ice Content of Crater at Moon's South Pole.* NASA's Lunar Reconnaissance Orbiter website. (http://www.nasa.gov/mission_pages/LRO/news/crater-ice.html)

6. Blackman, Eric G. Undated. *Tides and Gravitational Locking.* Astronomy 104 Solar System course, Univ. of Rochester, NY. (http://www.pas.rochester.edu/~blackman/ast104/tides.html)

7. Simanek, Donald E. 2011. *Tidal Misconceptions.* Lock Haven Univ. website. (https://www.lhup.edu/~dsimanek/scenario/tides.htm)

8. Touma, Jihad and Jack Wisdom. 1994. *Evolution of the Earth-Moon system.* The Astronomical Journal, vol. 108, no. 5, pp. 1943-1961. Harvard-Smithsonian Center for Astrophysics website. (http://adsabs.harvard.edu/cgi-bin/bib_query?1994AJ....108.1943T)

9. Blackman, Eric G. Undated. *Tides and Gravitational Locking.* Astronomy 104 Solar System course, Univ. of Rochester, NY. (http://www.pas.rochester.edu/~blackman/ast104/tidal.html)

10. Pogge, Richard. Undated. *Astronomy 161: An Introduction to Solar System Astronomy.* OH State Univ., Columbus. (http://www.astronomy.ohio-state.edu/~pogge/Ast161/Unit4/tides.html)

11. Touma, Jihad and Jack Wisdom. 1994.

12–13. Pogge, Richard. Undated.

14. McDonald. Kirk T. 2013. *Spin-Orbit Coupling in the Earth-Moon System.* Joseph Henry Laboratories, Princeton University, Princeton, NJ. (http://www.physics.princeton.edu/~mcdonald/examples/spin_orbit.pdf)

15. NASA. Undated. *Our Solar System: Moons.* Solar System Exploration website. (https://solarsystem.nasa.gov/planets/profile.cfm?Display=Moons)

16. Cain, Frasier. 2013. *How Many Moons Does Earth Have?* Universe Today website. (http://www.universetoday.com/15019/how-many-moons-does-earth-have/)

Chasing the Moon

1–2. Simanek, Donald E. 2010. *The Moon Illusion,*

An Unsolved Mystery. Lock Haven PA Univ. website. (http://www.lhup.edu/~dsimanek/3d/moonillu.htm)

3. Gallagher, Brian. 2014. *Your Brain Can't Handle the Moon.* Issue 019, Nautilus website. (http://nautil.us/issue/19/illusions/your-brain-cant-handle-the-moon)

Also see: L. Kaufman, et. al. 2007. *Perceptual distance and the moon illusion.* Spatial Vision, Vol. 20, No. 1–2, pp. 155–175. (http: //www.psych.nyu.edu/kaufman/perceptual_distance.pdf)

Night Visions

1. Berson, David M. 2003. *Strange vision: ganglion cells as circadian photoreceptors.* TRENDS in Neurosciences Vol.26 No.6, pp. 314-320.

2. Sargis, Robert M. 2014. *An Overview of the Pineal Gland.* Endocrineweb website. (http://www.endocrineweb.com/endocrinology/overview-pineal-gland)

3–4. Vandernoot, Eric. Undated. *How Light Pollution Affects Human Health.* FL Atlantic Univ. Dept. of Physics website. (http://physics.fau.edu/observatory/lightpol-health.html)

5. S. M. Pawson and M. K.-F. Bader. 2014. *LED lighting increases the ecological impact of light pollution irrespective of color temperature.* Ecological Applications 24:1561–1568.

6. Stevens et. al. 2013. *Adverse Health Effects of Nighttime Lighting.* American Journal of Preventive Medicine, 2013;45(3):343–346. (http://www.atmob.org/library/resources/AJPM13.pdf)

7. Stevens, R. G., Brainard, G. C., Blask, D. E., Lockley, S. W. and Motta, M. E. 2014. *Breast cancer and circadian disruption from electric lighting in the modern world.* CA: A Cancer Journal for Clinicians, 64: 207–218. doi: 10.3322/caac.21218 (http://onlinelibrary.wiley.com/doi/10.3322/caac.21218/full)

8. Chen, Eric. 2010. *Seeing Blue.* Nightscape Issue #80, DarkSky.org website. (http://www.darksky.org/assets/documents/SeeingBlue.pdf)

9. International Dark-Sky Association. 2010. *Visibility, Environmental, and Astronomical Issues Associated with Blue-Rich White Outdoor Lighting.* Tucson, AZ. 23 pp.

10. Keller, Britt. 2012. *The pineal gland, a link to our third eye.* Brain World website. (http://brainworldmagazine.com/the-pineal-gland-a-link-to-our-third-eye/)

Aurora Borealis ~ Light of the Northern Dancers

1. Lienhard, John. Undated. *Pierre Gassendi.* Engines of Our Engenuity website at Univ. of Houston.

2. Piegan Institute. 1996. *A Blackfoot Language Study.* Browning MT. (http://www.saokioheritage.com/AcrobatFiles/Holterman%20BF-English%20A-N.pdf)

3. McClintock, Walter. 1910. *The Old North Trail,* p. 487.

Macmillan and Co., London. 539 pp.

4. Canadian Space Agency. 2014. *The colours of the Northern Lights.* Govt. of Canada website. (http://www.asc-csa.gc.ca/eng/astronomy/auroramax/colours.asp)

5–6. Dunbar, Brian. 2006. *The History of Auroral Substorms.* NASA Auroras website. (http://www.nasa.gov/mission_pages/themis/auroras/substorm_history.html#.VPKdpvnF98E)

7–8. Fox, Karen. 2014. *The Science of Magnetic Reconnection.* NASA's Goddard Space Flight Center website. (http://www.nasa.gov/content/goddard/science-of-magnetic-reconnection/#.VPKgv_nF98G)

Air Glow Aurora

1. Cowley, Les. Undated. *Air Glow Formation.* Atomspheric Optics website. (http://www.atoptics.co.uk/highsky/airglow2.htm)

2. King, Bob. 2014. *How to See Airglow, the Green Sheen of Night.* Universe Today website. (http://www.universetoday.com/112237/how-to-see-airglow-the-green-sheen-of-night/)

3. Cowley, Les. Undated.

Milky Way Galaxy ~ The Wolf's Trail

1. Blackfoot Digital Library. Undated. *Makoyohsokoyi (Story of the Wolf Trail, a.k.a. Milky Way).* (http://blackfootdigital-library.com/en/asset/makoyohsokoyi-story-wolf-trail,-.k..-milky-way)

2. Canadian Heritage Information Network. Undated. *Makoi-Yohsokoyi - The Wolf Trail - The Milky Way.* (http://www.museevirtuel.ca/edu/ViewLoitDa.do?method=preview&lang=EN&id=5223#transcript)

3–4. Plait, Phil. 2010. *Alien clusters invade our galaxy!* From *Bad Astronomy* blog on Slate.com. (http://www.slate.com/blogs/bad_astronomy/2010/02/24/alien_clusters_invade_our_galaxy.html)

5. EarthSky.org. 2015. *How long would it take to get to Alpha Centauri?* (http://earthsky.org/space/alpha-centauri-travel-time).

6. Kaler, James. Undated. *The 170 Brightest Stars.* Univ. of IL *Stars* website.

7. Australia Telescope National Facility. Undated. *The Colour of Stars.* (http://www.atnf.csiro.au/outreach/education/senior/astrophysics/photometry_colour.html)

8. Grant, Madison. 1919. *Early History of Glacier National Park, Montana,* p. 4. Washington Govt. Printing Office. 12 pp.

Polaris ~ The Star That Stands Still

1. Holterman, Jack. 1985. *Place Names of Glacier/Waterton National Parks,* p. 87. Glacier Natural History Assoc., West Glacier, MT. 169 pp.

2. Piegan Institute. 1996. *A Blackfoot Language Study.* Browning MT. (http://www.saokioheritage.com/AcrobatFiles/Holterman%20BF-English%20A-N.pdf)

3. McClintock, Walter. 1910. *The Old North Trail,* p. 499. Macmillan and Co., London. 539 pp.

4. McClure, Bruce. 2014. *Thuban is a former Pole Star.* EarthSky.org website.

5. Anon. Undated. *Precession of the Equinox.* On W. WA Univ. *Astronomy 101* website. (http://www.wwu.edu/depts/skywise/a101_precession.html)

6. Shea, David. 2010. *Chief Mountain.* Thomas Printing. Kalispell, MT. 42 pp.

7. Miles, Kathy. Undated. *Draco the Dragon.* StarrySkies.com website. (http://starryskies.com/The_sky/constellations/draco.html)

8. Anon. Undated. *Draco Constellation.* Constellation-Guide.com website. (http://www.constellation-guide.com/constellation-list/draco-constellation/)

9. Anon. Undated. *Vega.* AstroPixels.com website. (http://astropixels.com/stars/Vega-01.html)

10. Solar System Quick. Undated. Vega Star. (http://www.solarsystemquick.com/universe/vega-star.htm)

11–12. Calculated using Stellarium planetarium. (http://www.stellarium.org/)

Big Dipper ~ Seven Brothers in the Great Bear

1. Bullchild, Percy. 1985. *The Sun Came Down. The History of the World as My Blackfeet Elders Told It.* Harper & Row. San Francisco, CA. 390 pp.

2. Canadian Heritage Information Network. Undated. *Ihkitsikammiksi - The Big Dipper.* (http://www.museevirtuel.ca/edu/ViewLoitDa.do?method=preview&lang=EN&id=5213)

3. Heavy Head, Ryan. 2010. *Solstice Eclipse and Aapohkiniiyi.* On AKAYO'KAKI A'PAWAAWAHKAA website. (http://akayokaki.blogspot.com/2010/12/solstice-eclipse-and-aapohkiniiyi.html)

4. Scriver, Mary Strachan. 2007. *Piegan Institute Ninth Annual History Conference.* Prairie Mary blogsite. (http://prairiemary.blogspot.com/2007/08/piegan-institute-ninth-annual-history.html)

5. Hungry Wolf, Adolf. *The Blackfoot Papers - Volume Two: Pikunni Ceremonial Life,* p. 335. Good Medicine Cultural Foundation. Skookumchuk, BC. 290 pp.

6. Canadian Heritage Information Network. Undated. *Ihkitsikammiksi - The Big Dipper.* (http://www.museevirtuel.ca/edu/ViewLoitDa.do;jsessionid=1C9E494E6D-29A0FA2315696258051973?method=preview&lang=EN&id=5213).

7. Wissler, Clark, and D.C. Duvall. 2007. *The Seven Stars,* in *Mythology of the Blackfoot Indians.* 2nd Edition. Univ. of NE Press. 166 pp.

8. Willows, Earl. Undated. *Earl Willows tells the story of The Seven Stars.* Blackfoot Digital Library website. (http://blackfootdigitallibrary.com/en/asset/earl-willows-tells-story-seven-stars)

9. Miles, Kathy. Undated. *Ursa Major.* StarrySkies.com website. (http://starryskies.com/The_sky/constellations/ursa_major.html)

10. Anon. Undated. *The Myths of Ursa Major, The Great Bear.* The American Association of Variable Star Observers website. (http://www.aavso.org/myths-uma)

11. Anon. 2013. *Ursa Major (great bear).* Chandra X-ray Observatory website. (http://chandra.harvard.edu/photo/constellations/ursamajor.html)

12. McClintock, Walter. 1910. *The Old North Trail,* p. 478. Macmillan and Co., London. 539 pp.

13. McClure, Bruce. 2014. *Big and Little Dippers: Everything you need to know.* EarthSky.org website. (http://earthsky.org/favorite-star-patterns/big-and-little-dippers-highlight-northern-sky)

Orion in the Sky

1. Hanna, Warren L. 1986. *The Life and Times of James Willard Schultz (Apikuni),* p. 138. Univ. of OK Press, Norman. 382 pp.

2. Hungry Wolf, Adolf. *Pikunni History and Culture - The Blackfoot Papers - Volume One,* p. 263. Good Medicine Cultural Foundation. Skookumchuk, BC. 290 pp.

3. International Astronomical Union. Undated. *The Constellations.* IAU website. (https://www.iau.org/public/themes/constellations/)

4. Rollins, Kathleen Flanagan. 2013. *Missing: Fierce, Powerful Goddess.* Misfits and Heroes website. (https://misfitsandheroes.wordpress.com/2013/08/20/missing-fierce-powerful-goddess/)

5. Kunitzsch, Paul and Tim Smart. 2006. *A Dictionary of Modern Star Names.* Sterling Pub Co Inc. New York, NY. 66 pp.

6. Brown, Laurel. 2009. *Betelgeuse, the history of a star name.* Examiner.com website. (http://www.examiner.com/article/betelgeuse-the-history-of-a-star-name)

7. Allen, Richard H. 1889. *Star Names: Their Lore and Meaning,* pp 305-320. Dover Publications (1963 revised edition), New York, NY. 563 pp.

8. McClure, Bruce. 2015. *Orion Nebula is a place where new stars are born.* EarthSky.org website.

9. Sessions, Larry. 2015. *Betelgeuse will explode someday.* On EarthSky.org website.

10. Upgren, Arthur. *Night Has a Thousand Eyes.* 2000. Basic Books. New York, NY. 320 pp.

11. Hubblesite.org. *Betelgeuse.* Undated. (http://hubblesite.org/explore_astronomy/black_holes/encyc_mod1_q5.html)

Pleiades ~ The Lost Boys

1. Moroney, Lynn. 2011. *Montana Skies, Blackfeet Astronomy, The Bunched Stars,* p. 23. MT Office of Public Instr., Helena. 38 pp.

2–3. McClintock, Walter. 1910. *The Old North Trail,* p. 490. Macmillan and Co., London. 539 pp.

4. Wissler, Clark, and D.C. Duvall. 1908. *The Bunched Stars,* p. 71, in *Mythology of the Blackfoot Indians.* 2nd Edition (2007). Univ. of NE Press.

5. Hungry Wolf, Adolf. 2006. *The Blackfoot Papers - Volume Three: Pikunni Portfolio Glacier National Park,* pages 722, 738. Good Medicine Foundation. Skookumchuk, BC. 1,524 pp.

6. Eggermont-Molenaar, Mary, ed. *Montana 1911: A professor and his wife among the Blackfeet,* p. 75. 2005. Univ. of Calgary Press, AB. 417 pp.

7–8. Anon. 2013. *Pleiades: The Seven Sisters (Messier 45).* Constellation Guide website. (http://www.constellation-guide.com/pleiades-the-seven-sisters-messier-45/)

A Star-Feeding

1. McClintock, Walter. 1910. *The Old North Trail,* p. 487. Macmillan and Co., London. 539 pp.

2. Choteau Acantha Newspaper. July 27, 1910. *An Unexpected Comet.* MT Memory Project website. (http://mt-memory.org/cdm/compoundobject/collection/p16013coll39/id/4401/rec/28)

3. The New York Times. Jan. 30, 1910. *Not Much is Known of Daylight Comet.* (http://query.nytimes.com/gst/abstract.html?res=9400E7D61730E233A25753C3A9679C946196D6CF)

4. Chamberlain, V. 1984. *Astronomical content of North American Plains Indian calendars,* p. S46. In *Archaeoastronomy* (U.K.), No. 6, p. S1 - S54. (http://adsabs.harvard.edu/full/1984JHAS...15....1C)

5. Anon. Undated. *Vital Statistics of Asteroids and Comets.* Science Clarified website. (http://www.scienceclarified.com/scitech/Comets-and-Asteroids/Vital-Statistics-of-Asteroids-and-Comets.html)

6. Orr, Kim. 2010. *Comet Facts for Students.* NASA Jet Propulsion Laboratory website. (http://www.jpl.nasa.gov/education/index.cfm?page=214)

7. Anon. Undated. *Jupiter-type comet.* The Worlds of David Darling Encyclopedia of Science website. (http://www.david-darling.info/encyclopedia/J/Jupitertype.html)

8. Garcia-Sanchez, Joan, et al. 1999. *Stellar encounters with the Oort Cloud based on "Hipparcos" data.* The Astronomical Journal, 117:1042-1055. (http://iopscience.iop.org/1538-3881/117/2/1042/fulltext/)

9 Anon. Undated. *Long-period comet.* The Worlds of David Darling Encyclopedia of Science website. (http://www.david-darling.info/encyclopedia/L/longperiod.html)

10. Mamajek, Eric E. et al. 2015. *The Closest Known Flyby of a Star to the Solar System.* The Astrophysical Journal Letters, Volume 800, Number 1. (ApJ 800 L17. doi:10.1088/2041-8205/800/1/L17)

11. Krupp, E.C. 1991. *Out of the Blue,* pp. 312-324, in *Beyond the Blue Horizon.* Harper Collins. New York, NY. 387 pp.

12. Ahrens, T.J., et. al. 1993. *Comet Shoemaker-Levy 9 Impact on Jovian Atmosphere.* American Astronomical Society, 25th DPS Meeting, #07.06; Bulletin of the American Astronomical Society, Vol. 25, p.1043.

13. European Space Agency. Undated. *Rosetta, Rendezvous with a comet.* (http://rosetta.esa.int/)

When Stars Fall

1. Chamberlain, V. 1984. *Astronomical content of North American Plains Indian calendars,* p. S46. In *Archaeoastronomy* (U.K.), No. 6, p. S1 - S54. (http://adsabs.harvard.edu/full/1984JHAS...15....1C)

2. Clark, Ella. 1966. *Burning Star Jumps Into a Lake,* pp. 95-96, in *Indian Legends from the Northern Rockies.* Univ. of OK Press, Norman. 350 pp.

3. The Flathead Courier. 1911. *Heavenly Visitor Makes Polson.* Volume 1, No. 21. MT Memory Project website. (http://mtmemory.org/cdm/compoundobject/collection/p16013coll16/id/793/rec/2)

4. Anon. 2005. *Daylight Fireball of August 10, 1972.* Internet Archive website. (http://web.archive.org/web/20050120051405/www.maa.agleia.de/Comet/Other/1972.html)

5. T. Montmerle et al. 2006. *Solar System Formation and Early Evolution: the First 100 Million Years.* Earth, Moon, and Planets, Volume 98, Issue 1-4, pp 39-95. (https://www-n.oca.eu/morby/papers/EMP1.pdf)

6. Cokinos, Christopher. 2009. *The Fallen Sky.* The Penguin Group. New York, NY. 518 pp.

7. HubbleSite.org. Undated. Frequently Asked Questions. (http://hubblesite.org/reference_desk/faq/all.php.cat=solarsystem)

8. Westenberg, Artemis. 2013. *Trojan Asteroids around Jupiter explained.* ExploreMare.org website. (http://www.exploremars.org/trojan-asteroids-around-jupiter-explained)

9. Sephton MA. 2002. *Organic compounds in carbonaceous meteorites.* Nat Prod Rep. 2002 Jun;19(3):292-311. Review. PubMed PMID: 12137279.

10. NASA. 2012. *NASA and University Researchers Find a Clue to How Life Turned Left.* NASA *Solar System* website. (http://www.nasa.gov/topics/solarsystem/features/life-turned-left.html)

11. Martins, Z. et al. 2013. *Shock synthesis of amino acids from impacting cometary and icy planet surface analogues.* Nature Geoscience 6, 1045–1049 (2013) doi:10.1038/ngeo1930. (http://www.nature.com/ngeo/journal/v6/n12/full/ngeo1930.html)

12. Graun, Ken. 2007. *What's out tonight?* Ken Press, Tucson, AZ. 400 pp.

13. Man, Ingrid, Akiko Nakamura, Tadashi Mukai, Eds. 2008. *Small Bodies in Planetary Systems / Edition 1,* pp. 135-36. Springer, New York, NY. 329 pp.

14. Cokinos, Christopher. 2009. *The Fallen Sky.* The Penguin Group. New York, NY. 518 pp.

15. Richardson, James. Undated. *Meteor FAQ's.* American Meteor Society website. (http://www.amsmeteors.org/meteor-showers/meteor-faq/)

16. Richardson, James. Undated.

17. Man, Ingrid, Akiko Nakamura, Tadashi Mukai, Eds. 2008.

18–19. Cokinos, Christopher. 2009.

Dusty Stars & Snowballs

1. Sephton MA. 2002. *Organic compounds in carbonaceous meteorites.* Nat Prod Rep. 2002 Jun;19(3):292-311. Review. PubMed PMID: 12137279.

2. NASA. 2012. *NASA and University Researchers Find a Clue to How Life Turned Left.* NASA *Solar System* website. (http://www.nasa.gov/topics/solarsystem/features/life-turned-left.html)

3. Martins, Z. et al. 2013. *Shock synthesis of amino acids from impacting cometary and icy planet surface analogues.* Nature Geoscience 6, 1045–1049 (2013) doi:10.1038/ngeo1930. (http://www.nature.com/ngeo/journal/v6/n12/full/ngeo1930.html)

4. Sullivant, Rosemary. 2003. *A 'Smoking Gun' for Dinosaur Extinction.* NASA Jet Propulsion Laboratory website. (http://www.jpl.nasa.gov/news/news.php?feature=8).

5. NASA Jet Propulsion Laboratory. Undated. *The Probability of Collisions with Earth.* (http://www2.jpl.nasa.gov/sl9/back2.html)

6. NASA Jet Propulsion Laboratory. Undated. *Near Earth Object Program.* (http://neo.jpl.nasa.gov/faq/)

7-8. Cokinos, Christopher. 2009. *The Fallen Sky.* The Penguin Group. New York, NY. 518 pp.

9. Cokinos, Christopher. 2009. Page 40.

10. Anon. 2010. Cree - *Whatever Happened to the Manito Stone?? Has it been returned?* Comment on *Native Quotes and Brilliance* website.

11–13. Spratt, C. E. *Canada's iron creek meteorite.* Journal of the Royal Astronomical Society of Canada (ISSN 0035-872X), vol. 83, April 1989, p. 81-91. (http://articles.adsabs.harvard.edu//full/1989JRASC..83...81S/0000084.000.html)

14. Gerson, Jen. 2012. *First Nations college calls for return of sacred meteorite from Alberta museum.* NationalPost.com. (http://news.nationalpost.com/2012/08/08/first-nations-college-calls-for-return-of-sacred-meteorite-from-alberta-museum/)

15. Baalke, Ron. Undated. *Mars Meteorites.* NASA Jet Propulsion Laboratory website. (http://www2.jpl.nasa.gov/snc/)

16. Korotev, Randy L. 2015. *List of Lunar Meteorites.* WA Univ., St. Louis, MO, Dept. of Earth and Planetary Sciences website. (http://meteorites.wustl.edu/lunar/moon_meteorites_list_alpha.htm)

17. Anon. 2013. *Montana Meteorites Map.* On *Meteorite Maps and Impact Craters - Worldwide* website. (http://worldwidemeteoritemaps.blogspot.com/2013/10/meteorite-map-of-montana.html)

18. O'Dale, Charles. Undated. *Beaverhead Impact Structure.* Royal Astronomical Society of Canada website. (http://ottawa-rasc.ca/wiki/index.php?title=Odale_beaverhead)

19. Holterman, Jack. 1985. *Place Names of Glacier/Waterton National Parks,* pp. 42-43. Glacier Natural History Assoc., West Glacier, MT. 169 pp.

Near-Earth Asteroids

1. NASA Near Earth Object Program. 2015. *Number of Known Accessible Near-Earth Asteroids Doubles Since 2010.* NASA Jet Propulsion Laboratory website. (http://neo.jpl.nasa.gov/news/news189.html)

2. Smithsonian Nat. Air and Space Museum. Undated. *Near-Earth Asteroids.* (https://airandspace.si.edu/exhibitions/exploring-the-planets/online/asteroids/AST_near.html)

3–5. NASA Jet Propulsion Laboratory. 2015. *Asteroid That Flew Past Earth Has Moon.* (http://www.jpl.nasa.gov/news/news.php?feature=4459)

Wandering Planets, & Son of Morning Star

1. Powell, Martin J. 2013. *Wandering Planets.* Naked Eye Planets website. (http://www.nakedeyeplanets.com/movements.htm)

2. McClintock, Walter. 1910. *The Old North Trail,* p. 491-500. Macmillan and Co., London. 539 pp.

3. Schultz, J.W. 1913. *The Story of Scarface,* Chapter VI in *Sinopah, the Indian Boy.* The Riverside Press, Riverside, MA. 155 pp.

4. Vest, Jay Hansford. 1988. *Traditional Blackfeet Religion and the Sacred Badger-Two Medicine Wildlands.* Journal of Law and Religion, Vol. 6, No. 2 (1988), pp. 455-489. Published by: Journal of Law and Religion, Inc.

5. Gladstone, Jack. 2015. Pers. comm.

6. Rao, Joe. 2012. *Venus and Jupiter Align: 3 Odd Facts About 2-Planet Tango*. Space.com website. (http://www.space.com/14852-venus-jupiter-alignment-facts.html)

7. Cain, Fraser. 2008. *Venus, the Morning Star and Evening Star*. Universe Today website. (http://www.universetoday.com/22570/venus-the-morning-star/)

8. Ventrudo, Brian. 2015. *The Art of Stargazing Month 1: Solar System The Planet Jupiter*. Mintaka Publishing Inc. 16 pp.

9. Redd, Nola Taylor. 2012. *How Big is Jupiter?* Space.com website. (http://www.space.com/18392-how-big-is-jupiter.html)

10. Plait, Phil. 1998. *A Failed Star, or Superplanet?* Bad Astronomy website. (http://www.badastronomy.com/bitesize/bd.html)

Eclipsed Realities

1. Chamberlain, V. 1984. *Astronomical content of North American Plains Indian calendars*, p. S49. In *Archaeoastronomy* (U.K.), No. 6, p. S1 - S54. (http://adsabs.harvard.edu/full/1984JHAS...15....1C)

2. Archive Society of Alberta. 2003. *Bull Plume's winter count*, Item iw-glen-22. (http://www.albertaonrecord.ca/iw-glen-22)

3. U.S. Naval Observatory. 1880. *Report of Col. Walter W DeLacy* (pp. 374-375), in *Reports on the Total Solar Eclipses of July 29, 1878, and January 11, 1880*. U.S. Government Printing Office. 426 pp.

4. Eddy, John. 1973. *The Great Eclipse of 1878*. Sky and Telescope, Vol. 45, No. 6.

5. Ferris, Timothy. 1988. *Coming of Age in the Milky Way*. Doubleday. New York, NY. 496 pp.

6. McGlaun, Dan. 2015. *Past American Eclipses*. Eclipse 2017 website. (http://www.eclipse2017.org/eclipse2017_main.htm)

7. Espenak, Fred. Undated. *Total Solar Eclipse of 1945 Jul 09* (interactive Google map). Eclipse Wise website. (http://eclipsewise.com/solar/SEgmap/1901-2000/SE1945Jul09T-gmap.html)

8. McGlaun, Dan. 2015.

9–10. Jubier, Xavier. 2015. *Solar Eclipses* (interactive Google map). (http://xjubier.free.fr/en/site_pages/solar_eclipses/TSE_2017_GoogleMapFull.html)

11. Espenak, Fred. *Solar Eclipse Preview: 2014 Through 2024*. Eclipse Wise website. (http://www.eclipsewise.com/solar/solar.html#preview)

Ursa Major Nocturne

1. Bartlebaugh, Chuck. 2012. *Be Bear Aware*. Center for Wildlife Information website. (http://www.centerforwildlifein-formation.org/BeBearAware/BearEncounters/bearencounters.html)

2. Get Bear Smart Society. Undated. *Play safe in bear habitat*. (http://www.centerforwildlifeinformation.org/BeBear-Aware/BearEncounters/bearencounters.html)

3. Emergency Essentials. 2014. *7 Signs You're Going to be Attacked by a Moose*. (http://beprepared.com/blog/15573/7-signs-youre-going-to-be-attacked-by-a-moose/)

4. Bartlebaugh, Chuck. 2012.

5. U.S. Forest Service. Undated. *Camping, Hiking & Hunting in Bear Country, Preventing Conflicts & Avoiding Confrontations*. (http://www.fs.usda.gov/Internet/FSE_DOCUMENTS/stelprdb5446564.pdf)

6. Tom Smith et al. 2008. *Efficacy of Bear Deterrent Spray in Alaska*. Journal of Wildlife Management 72(3):640–645.

7. Interagency Grizzly Bear Committee. 1999. *IGBC Bear Spray Position Paper*. (http://www.igbconline.org/images/pdf/1999_Bear_Spray_Position_Paper.pdf)

8. U.S. Fish & Wildlife Service. Undated. *Bear Spray vs. Bullets, Which offers better protection?* Fact Sheet No. 8. (http://www.fws.gov/mountain-prairie/species/mammals/grizzly/bear%20spray.pdf)

9. Natl. Park Service. *Using Bear Spray To Deter An Aggressive Bear*. Yellowstone Nat. Park website. (http://www.nps.gov/yell/learn/nature/bsdeter.htm)

Creatures of the Night

1. Vandernoot, Eric. Undated. *The Growth of "Just Another Light ..."* FL Atlantic Univ. Dept. of Physics website. (http://physics.fau.edu/observatory/lightpol-astro.html)

2. Narisada, Kohei and Duco Schreuder. 2004. *Light Pollution Handbook* (p. 133). Astrophysics and Space Science Library Series , #322. Springer Netherlands, Houten. 943 pp.

3. P. Cinzano et al. 2001. *Introduction* to, *The first World Atlas of the artificial night sky brightness*. Monthly Notices of the Royal Astronomical Society 328, 689–707. (http://www.lightpollution.it/cinzano/download/0108052.pdf)

4. Newman, Rhian. 2014. *Light pollution is bad for humans but may be even worse for animals*. The Conversation website. (http://theconversation.com/light-pollution-is-bad-for-humans-but-may-be-even-worse-for-animals-31144)

5. Catherine Rich & Travis Longcore (eds). 2006. *Effects of Artificial Night Lighting on Terrestrial Mammals*, pp. 15-42 in *Ecological Consequences of Artificial Night Lighting*. Island Press. Covelo, CA. 458 pp.

6. Franz Holker et al. 2010. *The dark side of light: a transdisciplinary research agenda for light pollution policy*. Ecology and Society 15(4): 13. (http://www.ecologyandsociety.org/vol15/iss4/art13/)

7. American Medical Assoc. Resolution 516. 2009. *Advocating and Support for Light Pollution Control Efforts and Glare Reduction for Both Public Safety and Energy Savings*. (http://www.eficienciaenergetica.gub.uy/archivo/documents/material_interes/AmericanMedicalAssociation%20_Resolution516.pdf)

8. DeNoon, Daniel. 2003. *Bright Light at Night Linked to Increased Cancer Risk*. Web MD website. (http://www.webmd.com/breast-cancer/news/20030714/hormone-melatonin-slows-breast-cancer)

9. American Cancer Society. 2015. *What are the risk factors for breast cancer?* Am. Cancer Soc. website. (http://www.cancer.org/cancer/breastcancer/detailedguide/breast-cancer-risk-factors)

10. Frank, Kenneth. 2006. *Effects of Artificial Lighting on Moths*, pp. 305-344. Chapter 13 in *Ecological Consequences of Artificial Night Lighting*. Catherine Rich & Travis Longcore (eds). Island Press. Covelo, CA. 458 pp.

11-12. Adam J. Vanbergen et al. 2014. *Status and value of pollinators and pollination services*. Dept. for Environment, Food & Rural Affairs. London.

13. Lloyd, James. 2006. *Stray Light, Fireflies, and Fireflyers*, pp. 345-364. Chapter 14 in *Ecological Consequences of Artificial Night Lighting*. Catherine Rich & Travis Longcore (eds). Island Press. Covelo, CA. 458 pp.

14. A. Rand et al. 1997. *Light Levels Influence Female Choice in Tungara Frogs: Predation Rick Assessment?* Copeia, pp. 447-450. (http://www.sbs.utexas.edu/ryan/Publications/1997/1997Copeia97-447.pdf)

15. Marcu Byrne et al. 2002. *Visual cues used by ball-rolling dung beetles for orientation*. J Comp Physiol A (2003) 189: 411–418. DOI 10.1007/s00359-003-0415-1. (http://www.wits.ac.za/files/res2a45e25994904a58ac969cc935e20d3f.pdf)

16. Miller, Mark. 2006. *Apparent Effects of Light Pollution on Singing Behavior of American Robins*. The Condor Feb 2006 : Vol. 108, Issue 1, pg(s) 130-139 doi: 10.1650/0010-5422(2006)108[0130:AEOLPO]2.0.CO;2.

17–18. Chaney, William R. 2002. *Does Night Lighting Harm Trees?* FNR-FAQ-17, Department of Forestry and Natural Resources, Purdue University, West Lafayette, IN.

19. Vandernoot, Eric. Undated. *Light Pollution Hurts Our Economy and Our Resources*. FL Atlantic Univ. Dept. of Physics website. (http://physics.fau.edu/observatory/light-pol-econ.html)

20. Vandernoot, Eric. Undated. *Light Pollution Endangers Our Security and Our Safety*. FL Atlantic Univ. Dept. of Physics website. (http://physics.fau.edu/observatory/light-pol-security.html)

21. Vandernoot, Eric. Undated. *FBI Residential Burglary Crime Statistics for 2004 - 2013*. FL Atlantic Univ. Dept. of

Physics website. (http://physics.fau.edu/observatory/light-pol-security.html#FBICrimeStats)

22. Stevens, Richard G., et. al. 2014. *Breast cancer and circadian disruption from electric lighting in the modern world.* CA: A Cancer Journal for Clinicians, 64: 207–218. doi: 10.3322/caac.21218.

23. American Cancer Society. 2015.

24. Kloog, Itai et al. *Does the Modern Urbanized Sleeping Habitat Pose a Breast Cancer Risk?* Feb., 2011, Vol. 28, No. 1 , Pages 76-80 (doi:10.3109/07420528.2010.531490).

Mountain Moonsets

1. Elrod, Morton. 1924. *Elrod's guide and book of information of Glacier National Park.* The Missoulian Publishing Company. Missoula, MT. 208 pp.

2. Dennison, Eric. 2012. *Morton J. Elrod: Glacier Park Naturalist.* Univ. of MT Crown of the Continent Dispatches, Issue 2, p. 2. (http://crown-yellowstone.umt.edu/E-Publications/Crown%20of%20the%20Continent%20Dispatches_Volume%202_Autumn%202012.pdf)

3. The Northwest Digital Archives. Undated. *Biographical Note,* in *Guide to the Morton J. Elrod Papers 1885-1959.* (http://nwda.orbiscascade.org/ark:/80444/xv45831)

4. The Northwest Digital Archives. Undated.

5. The Northwest Digital Archives. Undated.

6. Dennison, Eric. 2012, p. 8.

7. Djuff, Ray and Chris Morrison. 2010. *Waterton and Glacier in a Snap!: Fast Facts and Titillating Trivia,* p. 69. Rocky Mountain Books, Calgary, AB. 240 pp.

8. Grinnell, G.B. 1892. *Blackfoot Lodge Tales,* p. 259. Charles Scribner's Sons, New York, NY. 310 pp.

9. Schultz, James W. 1926. *Signposts of Adventure: Glacier National Park as the Indians Know it,* pp. 107-108. Houghton Mifflin Co., Boston, MA.224 pp.

10. Holterman, Jack. 1985. *Place Names of Glacier/Waterton National Parks,* p. 62. Glacier Natural History Assoc., West Glacier, MT. 169 pp.

Solar Rays & Moon Beams

1. Red Crow College Dept. of Kainai Studies. Undated. *Greetings.* Cardston AB. (http://kainaistudies.com/modules/phraseology/playcat.php?cid=1)

2. Peterson, Sarah. 2010. *A Beginning Course in Colville-Okanagan Salish.* Salish School of Spokane, WA. (http://www.interiorsalish.com/images/nselxcin_1_book.pdf)

3. Atmospheric Optics. Undated. *Rays and Shadows.* (http://www.atoptics.co.uk/rayshad.htm)

Painting on Clouds

1. Natl. Weather Service. Undated. *Ten Basic Cloud Types.* (http://www.srh.noaa.gov/srh/jetstream/clouds/cloudwise/types.html)

2. Grant, Madison. 1919. *Early History of Glacier National Park, Montana,* p. 11. WA Govt. Printing Office. 12 pp.

Returning to the Sun

1. Schultz, James W. 1926. *Signposts of Adventure: Glacier National Park as the Indians Know it,* p. 118. Houghton Mifflin Co., Boston, MA.224 pp.

2–4. Holterman, Jack. 1985. *Place Names of Glacier/Waterton National Parks,* p. 56. Glacier Natural History Assoc., West Glacier, MT. 169 pp.

5. Kipp, Darrell Robes. 2010. *Introduction,* p. 6, in *The Sun God's Children* by J.W. Schultz. Riverbend Publishing, Helena, MT. 259 pp.

6. Djuff, Ray and Chris Morrison. 2010. *Waterton and Glacier in a Snap!: Fast Facts and Titillating Trivia,* p. 105. Rocky Mountain Books, Calgary, AB. 240 pp.

7. Schultz, James Willard. 1907. *My Life as an Indian.* Fawcett Publications, Greenwich, CT. 426 pp.

8. Hungry Wolf, Adolf. *The Blackfoot Papers - Volume One,* p. 261. Good Medicine Cultural Foundation. Skookumchuck, BC. 290 pp.

9. Schultz, James W. 1926. Page 15.

10. Grinnell, G.B. 1892. *Blackfoot Lodge Tales,* p. xiii. Charles Scribner's Sons, New York, NY. 310 pp.

11-12. Kipp, Darrell Robes. 2010. *Introduction,* p. 6, in *The Sun God's Children* by J.W. Schultz. Riverbend Publishing, Helena, MT. 259 pp.

13. Schultz, James W. 1926. Page 4.

14. Schultz, James W. 1926. Page 126.

15. Schultz, James W. 1926. Pp. 6-7.

16. Hanna, Warren L. 1986. *The Life and Times of James Willard Schultz (Apikuni),* p. 229. Univ. of OK Press, Norman. 382 pp.

17. Schultz, James W. 1926. Page 117.

18. Holterman, Jack. 1985. Page 56.

19. Schultz, James W. 1926. Page 118.

20. Lagayette, Pierre, Ed. 2006. *Nature et progrès: interactions, exclusions, mutations,* p. 55. Univ. of Paris Press, Sorbonne. 329 pp.

21. Robinson, Donald. 1960. *Historic Place Names,* in *Through The Years in Glacier National Park.* Glacier Natural

History Association, Inc. Bulletin No. 8. West Glacier, MT. (http://www.cr.nps.gov/history/online_books/glac/appa.htm)

22. Passmore, Blake. 2014. *What They Called It: Stories of Glacier's Names Along Going-To-The-Sun Road.* Montana Outdoor Guidebooks, Kalispell, MT. 112 pp.

23. Wikipedia. 2015. James Willard Schultz. (http://en.wikipedia.org/wiki/James_Willard_Schultz#cite_ref-Hanna_1-4)

24. Kipp, Darrell Robes. 2010, p. 7.

25. Holterman, Jack. 1985. Pages 13, 14, 94.

26. Holterman, Jack. 1985. Page 126.

Caution Lights & Progress

1. Duriscoe, Dan. 2001. *Preserving Pristine Night Skies in National Parks and the Wilderness Ethic.* The George Wright Society Forum. Volume 18, Number 4, pp. 30-36. Hancock, MI.

2. Albers, Steve and Dan Duriscoe. 2001. *Modeling Light Pollution from Population Data and Implications for National Park Service Lands.* George Wright Society Forum. Volume 18, Number 4, pp. 56-68.

3. Lorenz, David. *Light Pollution Atlas 2006.* Univ. of WI, Madison (http://djlorenz.github.io/astronomy/lp2006/)

4. The Glacier Park Conservancy. 2014. *Half the Park Happens After Dark,* p. 6 in *The 2015 field guide to park project priorities.* 40 pp.

5. International Dark-Sky Assoc. Undated. *International Dark-Sky Parks.* (http://www.darksky.org/international-dark-sky-places/about-ids-places/parks)

6. Natl. Park Service. 2009. *The Night Sky Program.* (http://www.nationalparkstraveler.com/files/Night_Sky_Program_Brief.pdf)

Basics of Dark-Sky-Friendly Lighting

1. Ekirch, A. Roger. 2005. *Part II: Laws of Nature,* in *At Day's Close, Night in Times Past.* W.W. Norton & Co., New York, NY. 447 pp.

2. International Dark-Sky Association. 2010. *Visibility, Environmental, and Astronomical Issues Associated with Blue-Rich White Outdoor Lighting.* Tucson, AZ. 23 pp.

3. International Dark Sky Association. Undated. *Directory of Lighting Ordinances.* (http://darksky.org/education/35-ida/outdoor-lighting/81-other-ordinances)

4. Neugent, Kathryn F. and Philip Massey. *The Spectrum of the Night Sky Over Kitt Peak: Changes Over Two Decades.* Publications of the Astronomical Society of the Pacific, Vol. 122, No. 896 (October 2010), pp. 1246-1253.

EPILOGUE

Be humble but not timid. To be humble is to connect yourself to the stars and the entire universe and makes you aware there is something unique about life that is to be enjoyed without fear. We are people from the stars, and because of it we are sacred.

–Official website of the Blackfoot Nation

When I go outside at night,
And look up and the stars are bright.
Sometimes I lay on the ground,
And imagine that the sky is down.
And if the Earth should then let go,
I'd fall into the stars below,
I'd fall into the stars below...

–Lyrics from "The Play" by Peter Mayer

"I placed my blanket-bed on the prairie-grass, and, instead of the lodge covering for a roof, I had the magnificent canopy of the night-sky, spangled with an innumerable multitude of stars. On account of the clearness of the atmosphere over the plains, these sparkling orbs of light shone with a rare brilliance and splendour, and appeared lower down in the horizon than I had ever seen elsewhere. Lying on my back and gazing up into the wonderful beauty of the heavens gave me an overwhelming sense of the infinity of God's universe and my own littleness by comparison."

–Walter McClintock ~ camped among the Blackfeet near East Glacier, Montana 1895